MW00587401

DAY HIKES FROM THE RIVER

A guide to 100 hikes from camps on the Colorado River in Grand Canyon National Park

Copyright 1999, 2002, 2006 Tom Martin
ISBN 0-9674595-9-1
Printed in China

Vishnu Temple Press
O. Box 30821 Flagstaff, AZ 86003
(928) 556-0742
www.vishnutemplepress.com

Cover and photo design by Dierker Design
Cover photos copyright by Tom Martin
Third Edition 2007 Vishnu Temple Press

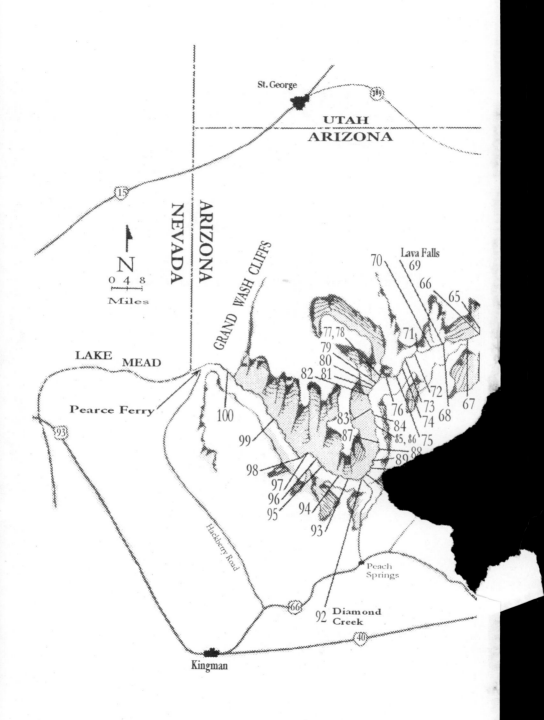

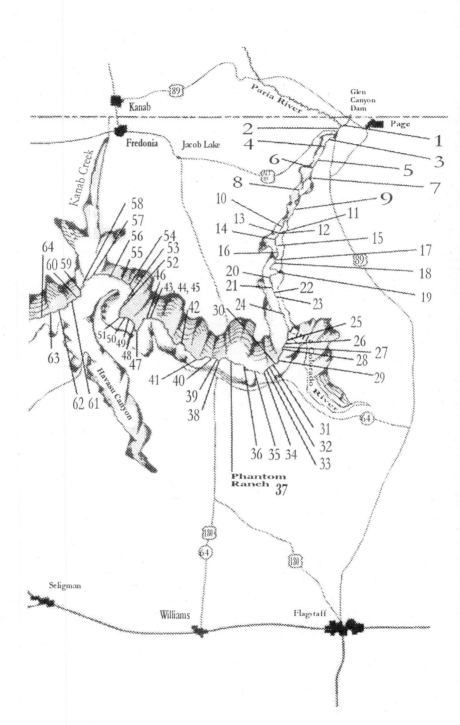

Paria River

Glen
Canyon
Dam

89   Kanab

Page

Fredonia   Jacob Lake

2
4

1

6

5
3

8

7

Kanab Creek

89

9

10

13
14

11

12

15

16

20
21

17

18

89

19

24

22

23

58

57

56

55

54
53
52

46

43, 44, 45

42

30

25

26
28

27

29

64
60 59

51 50 49

48
47

41 40

39

38

31
32
33

63

Havasu Canyon

62 61

36 35 34

Colorado River

64

Phantom
Ranch 37

180

64

180

Seligman

Williams

Flagstaff

A Brief Note On Safety In Grand Canyon

The Grand Canyon is a very dangerous place. Hiking, climbing and river running all have certain dangers and hazards accompanying them.

Such risks, dangers and hazards include but are in no way limited to drowning, not drinking enough water, drinking too much water, coming in contact with poisonous wildlife, falling, being caught in a flash flood, being hit by falling rock, being exposed to hazardous conditions during stream crossings, suffering from heat exhaustion, suffering from heat stroke, and being exposed to often rapidly changing weather conditions including lightning, snow, and flooding, any and all of which may cause injury or death.

The author, editor and publisher of this guide can in no way ensure the safety of any hike, camp or activity mentioned in this guide. Conditions change suddenly, quickly and constantly in Grand Canyon. Travelers in Grand Canyon National Park should always contact the Grand Canyon River Permits Office and the Grand Canyon Backcountry Office in Grand Canyon National Park for current conditions and permits before traveling in Grand Canyon National Park.

For the latest information on conditions in the park, contact:

Grand Canyon National Park
Backcountry Permits Office
(928) 638-7875
River Permits Office
(800) 959-9164
(928) 638-7843
P.O. Box 129
Grand Canyon, AZ 86023

This guide does not replace the skills necessary to safely travel on the Colorado River and through the backcountry in Grand Canyon National Park. Rapidly changing conditions in Grand Canyon will ensure the information in this book will be out of date before the ink on this page is dry. The hikes in this book are suggestions. Readers of this book are reminded there is no substitute for your own common sense, skill and understanding of route finding, climbing, river rafting and exploring in Grand Canyon National Park.

Table Of Contents

PREFACE

This book is written to aid the knowledge base of all river travelers in Grand Canyon National Park. An ever-growing number of the world's citizens are becoming aware of the need to be active stewards in the protection of the world's great natural treasures in our national parks. If our national parks are to be preserved for future generations while remaining accessible to the broadest spectrum of the population, the price of equitable access will be resource protection and the dissemination of knowledge currently held only by the few. It is hoped that this guidebook will assist in this stewardship.

ACKNOWLEDGEMENTS

Thanks for this third edition go to Greg Reiff, Dr. Tom Myers, Duwain Whitis, Dena Kuhn, Doug Nering and the folks at North Country Community Health Center Grand Canyon Clinic.

Hiking all of the hikes in this book has been made more enjoyable by the many wonderful folks I have been privileged to explore the Grand Canyon with. Special thanks to Aaron Tomasi, Claudia Bakula, Wayne Ball, Bronze Black and his wonderful little penlight that saved Wayne, Bronze and I on our descent after climbing Vishnu Temple, Bryan Wisher, Kim Rapson, Dr. Tom Myers, Pam Foti, Ivo Lucchitta, Doug Porter, Paul Lastayo, Linda Mazzu, Eric Christensen, Guy Cloutier, Amanda Gibbon, Dan Cassidy, Glen Doster, Jeanie Haney, Gary Ladd, Cecelia Mortenson, Larry Stevens, Michelle Madland, Dave Mortenson, Ed Smith, Mary Pat Zitzer, Alan Kesselheim, Marcy DeMillion, Josh Burgel, Cale Shaffer, May Lee, Arnie Richards, Jeff Ingram, Jason Wesley, Zander Brown, Jessie Plotnick, Tom Pendley, John Middendorf, Michael Stock, Jocelyn Gibbon, Mike Thompson, Mrill Ingram, Ken Agnew, Tom Robey, Gail Ryba, Wendy Fuge, Mark Fuge and the best hiking partner I've ever had the good fortune to walk with, Hazel Clark.

NOTE

This book is intended for use with the waterproof **Guide to the Colorado River in the Grand Canyon** by Tom Martin and Duwain Whitis. Vishnu Temple Press, www.vishnutemplepress.com PO Box 30821, Flagstaff, AZ 86003-0821 or RiverMaps, www.rivermaps.net 1540 S. Turnersville Rd., Buda, Texas 78610.

INTRODUCTION

It has not been easy to compile a brief description of hikes that start from the water's edge in Grand Canyon National Park. Most hikers in the Canyon start their journey from the rim, carrying heavy backpacks and lots of water, and many books have been written describing the routes to be taken in this manner. Backpackers will certainly find this text helpful in its description of many backcountry routes. What is unique is that this is the first book to introduce the reader to day hikes that start from the Colorado River in Grand Canyon National Park. The text is written for the river runner who wants to go for a walk from the river with a fanny pack and a few quarts of water. The difficulty in compiling this work has been in the sheer size of the park and the necessity of personally exploring all of the hikes in this book in the very limited amount of time river trips afford for exploring.

This is in no way a complete list of all of the hikes possible on a river trip. With 2,000 square miles and 1.2 million acres of country out there in Grand Canyon National Park, consider this an introduction only to the vast possibilities available for Canyon hiking from the river. One important point to keep in mind as you float through the Grand Canyon is time. There is never enough of it! However much of this magical place that you can possibly see, experience and explore in any one river trip will never be enough. Be ready to let things go. This little book took many river trips worth of hiking to compile.

SYMBOLS, TERMS, TOOLS AND TIMES

Each hike in this guide is accompanied by a map. Each map includes the name of the hike associated with the map, a scale for computing distances, and an arrow that indicates north. A dotted line represents the described route. An arrow with the word FLOW written in it denotes the way the river flows and black triangles represent possible campsites. The words VERY DIFFICULT will occasionally be written on a map, with an arrow pointing to a specific spot or two. This means what it says.

Hikes in this guide are ranked as easy, difficult and very difficult. Very difficult routes may have exposure to falling long distances, may require climbing and may require covering a lot of uneven country, all in the same hike. Difficult hikes may require climbing and covering long distances in uneven country, while easy hikes may require some climbing and hiking long distances, usually over fairly easy terrain. Please note that a number of these hikes are very difficult and strenuous. Don't forget that you can turn back at any time. You may find that hikes classified as easy are very difficult for you. You may find that hikes classified as very difficult are very easy for you. This will all depend on your skill level at hiking off-trail in rugged terrain.

When in a drainage and the route description mentions creek right or left, this is ALWAYS facing downstream. No distances mentioned in this book have been measured with a distance meter. If you want it exact, bring along a surveyor. Distances are also measured in a straight level line. This will pose problems on many hikes when there is a few-thousand-foot gain in a simple half-mile of level distance.

River mile locations match *Guide To the Colorado River in the Grand Canyon*, by Tom Martin and Duwain Whitis, and it is recommended that the guide be used in conjunction with this book. See page viii for ordering information. River camp mileage matches NPS campsite mileage as much as possible. A compass will help you get around in the Canyon if you are not sure of your bearings.

The times mentioned to complete hikes in this guide are estimates. You may need more or less time than mentioned. Almost all of the routes described are off-trail. Most hikers who frequent Grand Canyon follow well-used trails and may need much more time to walk routes that have no trail to follow.

If you are on a loop hike, turning back may not be an option. When thinking about hiking a loop, give due consideration to the time of year, current weather conditions and your personal fitness level. Always let other members of your group know where you are going and when you are intending to return. Many hikers find hiking up a steep slope easier than climbing down one. If this describes you, then exercise caution in your hikes. Never climb up a route you don't think you can climb down.

It's essential to take a small first aid kit and enough water and food on any hike. In the summertime, plan on carrying and drinking a quart of water for every hour you are out hiking, and plan to accompany all that water drinking with eating salty snack foods hourly as well. Never start a long hike on an empty stomach. If you find the going too difficult, you should turn back.

Finally, please recognize that in Grand Canyon, things change. Sometimes, a lot! Beaches come and go, cliff faces peel off and cause landslides, and trails get swept away. Please let me know of errors in the text and maps, and of changes you see happen. It will make the next printing, if there ever is one, all the more accurate.

GEOLOGY

Hiking in Grand Canyon is a lot easier if you understand the basics of the geological terrain. Certain rock units are very easy to hike in, while others will pose difficult barriers to travel. The Redwall Limestone and Coconino Sandstone are the thickest continual cliffs you will have to deal with in the Canyon, while the Hermit Shale and Toroweap Formation are almost always easy to get around in.

Kaibab Limestone, with the Toroweap Formation just below it, forms the rim of the Canyon. Only in the very east end of Grand Canyon will the Kaibab and Toroweap form shear continuous cliffs. In most of the rest of the park, numerous routes through these two units will be found. The Coconino Sandstone, just below the Toroweap, can form a solid shear cliff over 350 feet high. Fortunately, the Coconino is very susceptible to faulting. The dozen hikes in this book that go through the Coconino are following watercourses, faults or ridgelines.

Below the Coconino is the Hermit Shale. The very soft and easily eroded Hermit Shale overlies the Esplanade. The term Esplanade is used to describe the topmost layer of the Supai Group, a cliff- and slope-forming shale and sandstone rock unit with four layers. These layers are the Esplanade, Wescogame, Manakacha and Watahomigi. The Supai can be maddening to get through, as it will be completely broken down in some spots, and a formidable cliff-slope-cliff-slope in other areas, typically where you most want to go. You will usually find a wide platform on top of the Supai, assuming you can find a way through the layers below.

Beneath the Supai is the Redwall. In this book, the term Redwall is used to describe a band of limestone cliffs actually comprised of a series of four rock units, the Redwall Limestone, Temple Butte Limestone, Undivided Dolomites and Muav Limestone. The Redwall will be with you on your river trip as a massive cliff from river mile 26. The Redwall is susceptible to faulting. Chutes through the otherwise impregnable Redwall will most often be in fault zones.

Below the Redwall is the soft Bright Angel Shale, and below that the Tapeats Sandstone. The term Tonto refers to the top of the Tapeats Sandstone from the Little Colorado River (Mile 61.5) to Elves Chasm (Mile 116.5). This broad bench is an enjoyable place for a stroll anytime you can get to it through the Tapeats cliffs below. The Tapeats will form a bench again below Pumpkin Springs (Mile 213.0). The normally crumbly Tapeats Sandstone will more often than not form a difficult band of cliffs. Look for chimneys and faults as a way through this rock layer. The Tapeats has one important drawback. When wet, it becomes very unstable and deadly. Please keep this in mind.

GRAND CANYON ROCK LAYERS

The following is a schematic of the Grand Canyon rock layers, as seen through the eyes of a day hiker.

Moenkopi
Sandstone

You will not encounter Moenkopi except at Lees Ferry and a few other select points.

.... This is the rim of the Canyon.

Kaibab
Limestone

Usually broken routes can be found through the Kaibab. Can sometimes form white cliffs.

Toroweap
Formation

The Toroweap is almost always an easy slope.

Coconino
Sandstone

Ugh. Look for faults through this white cliff.

Hermit
Shale

The red Hermit Shale is almost always an easy slope.

.... This bench is the Esplanade.

Supai
Group

The red Supai has banded cliffs with slopes. The bands can be hard to get through.

Redwall
Limestone

The Redwall is a gray cliff stained red by the mud of the Supai and Hermit above. Ugh here too. Look for faults.

Bright Angel
Shale

The gray-green Bright Angel offers easy going.

This bench is called the Tonto Platform in the upper Canyon.

Tapeats
Sandstone

The buff Tapeats Cliffs are deadly when wet. Look for plentiful chutes and chimneys.

The Grand Canyon Super Group
including the Diabase Sill

The Super Group comes in a wide array of colors. The black-gray Schist and pink Granite are steep.

Vishnu Schist and Zoroaster Granite

\ --------- Colorado River.

Below the Tapeats are the two rock units, the Grand Canyon Super Group above the Vishnu Schist and Zoroaster Granite. The Super Group consists of hardened sandstone, mudstone and siltstone. These strata are different than the Supai Group in that the Super Group shale's and sandstone's have been cooked and compressed just a bit deep with the earth's crust. This heating has made these rocks harden, and the resultant slopes they form are not easy to get a foothold on. Side sloping on the Super Group can in places be like walking on a sheet of plywood, tilted at an angle and covered with BB's. This can be most disconcerting when there is a drop below. The Super Group also contains the occasional lava band, either vertical like you'll see at Lava Chuar Canyon, at an angle like at Hance Rapid on river right, or horizontal like at Stone Creek. The Super Group represents over 12,000 feet of deposited rock. Even so, it is not always present between the Tapeats Sandstone above it and the Vishnu Schist below because it has been entirely eroded away.

Below the Super Group is the bedrock of the Grand Canyon, and most of North America for that matter. The Vishnu Schist is a very steep slope or cliff forming schist, intertwined with the pink or white Zoroaster Granite. This rock unit is very sharp and unforgiving if you slip while climbing through it.

ARCHEOLOGY AND RESOURCE PROTECTION

For the last 10,000 years or more, people have been hiking in and out of the Grand Canyon. Virtually every trail, route or game path was used by "those who came before." Evidence of these early Canyon hikers is everywhere in Grand Canyon. Archaeological sites, structures, artifacts, even the trails you walk, show the hand of man, dating back before the cradle of western civilization in some cases. Noticing these remains and thinking about the sandaled feet that may have walked these ways before you can do much to enhance your Canyon experience; but you should keep the following in mind as well.

All archeological sites and artifacts on federal lands are protected by federal law. Please respect these locations as the shrines they are. Do not touch or disturb what you do find. This includes not entering sites or sitting on structures. Many people respect Grand Canyon as the open-air shrine it is. Please do NOT build your own shine here, except in your mind. Remember the wonderful word, humility. You will be violating the Antiquities Act of 1906 and the Archeological Resource Protection Act of 1979 if you remove historical material that is greater then 50 years old. If you are in doubt about the age of anything you find in the Canyon, leave it alone.

It is of utmost importance that the Canyon hiker be mindful of how to hike in the fragile desert Canyon environment. Wherever there is a game path, trail or even the slightest trace of a route, use it. Try to walk in streambeds, on rock outcrops or up bouldery scree slopes. These areas are called durable surfaces. Hiking on these surfaces causes much less impact than hiking on dune surfaces or in soft talus slopes. The fragile desert plants do not take kindly to being stepped on, so avoid treading on them. Even the surface of the very soil itself is alive with microbiotic plants, moss and bacteria. This living ground cover helps hold the soil together. Your careless footsteps will instantly destroy this incredibly fragile life-form.

Keep in mind the large number of river runners who pass through the Canyon every year. You and 26,000 other folks are going to be camping, hiking, bathing, going to the bathroom and bumping into each other here in this open-air shrine annualy. This number of folks is probably more than were here in any single 250-year period before 1540. While at camp or stopped for lunch or a side hike, pee directly into the water of the Colorado River. If you are hiking up a side tributary, then hike at least 100 feet away from any water source to pee. Plan ahead, so you can pee into the Colorado River before your hike. Coordinate with other river trips around you so that everyone finds a campsite for the night. Clean up all the big and small pieces of trash at your camp. Good housekeeping keeps the ants far away from your camp. That means the scorpions will be far away too, out looking for ants. The mice will be far away looking for scorpions, and rattlesnakes will be far away looking for mice.

NATIVE AMERICAN LANDS

Grand Canyon National Park is bordered by three distinct Native American sovereign nations. Permission to hike on or across tribal lands should be obtained in advance. Where appropriate, the hikes in this book will alert you to the approximate border between park and tribal land. The following is a list of the tribal nations you may find yourself hiking in.

Havasupai Nation,
Havasupai Tourist Enterprises
P.O. Box 160, Supai, AZ 86435

Hualapai Nation,
Hualapai Grand Canyon Enterprises
P.O. Box 538, Peach Springs, AZ 86434

Navajo Nation
Navajo Parks and Recreation
P.O. Box 459, Cameron, AZ 86020

TOPOGRAPHICAL MAP INDEX

The following is a list of USGS 7.5' topographical maps and the hikes that go through the territory in each map:

Lees Ferry 1, 2 Navajo Bridge 2, 3 Bitter Springs 4, 5, 6 Emmett Wash 6, 7, 8 North Canyon Point 8, 9, 10, 11, 12, 13, 14 Buffalo Tank 14 Tatahatso Point 14, 15, 16, 19 Buffalo Ranch 17, 18 Point Imperial 20, 21 Nankoweap Mesa 21, 22, 23, 24 Cape Solitude 24, 25, 26, 27, 28 Desert View 28, 29, 30, 31 Cape Royal 30, 32, 33, 34, 35 Phantom Ranch 35, 36, 37 Grand Canyon 38, 39, 40, 41 Shiva Temple 38, 42 Havasupai Point 43, 44, 45 King Arthur Castle 43, 44 Explorers Monument 46, 47, 48 Powell Plateau 46, 52, 53, 54 Topocoba Hilltop 49 Fossil Bay 50, 51, 56 Tapeats Amphitheater 54 Fishtail Mesa 55, 56, 57 Kanab Point 57 Havasu Falls 58, 59, 61 S B Point 60, 61, 62 Fern Glen Canyon 62, 63, 64, 65 Gateway Rapids 63, 65, 66 Yunosi Point 63 Vulcans Throne 67, 68, 69 Whitmore Rapids 70, 71, 72 Vulcans Throne SW 73, 74, 75 Whitmore Point SE 76, 77, 78, 79 Whitmore Point SE 80, 81 Whitmore Point SW 80 Granite Park 82, 83, 84, 85, 86, 87 Diamond Peak 88, 89, 90, 91, 92 Diamond Creek 92 Peach Springs NE 92 Travertine Rapids 93, 94 Peach Springs Canyon 93 Separation Canyon 95, 96, 97 Amos Point 97, 98 Devils Slide Rapids 97 Bat Cave 99 Quartermaster Canyon 99 Columbine Falls 100

ABOUT THE AUTHOR

Tom Martin has been hiking in Grand Canyon from river rafting trips since 1969. He has participated in scientific rafting trips as a field technician, worked as a commercial river guide, and participated on non-commercial rafting trips as a permit holder. With multiple first ascents through the Redwall Limestone and numerous ascents of Grand Canyon named buttes on day hikes from the river, the author has hiked enough of Grand Canyon to be able to say "Of the cat that is Grand Canyon, I have seen one hair." Tom co-founded the Grand Canyon Private Boaters Association, the Grand Canyon Hikers and Backpackers Association, and presently serves as Co-Director of River Runners For Wilderness. Tom currently works as a physical therapist at the North Country Community Health Center Grand Canyon Clinic at the South Rim.

1. Lees Ferry, Lee's Backbone and the Spencer Trail

Both sides of the Colorado River at Lees Ferry offer boaters a lot of interesting country to hike around in. If you have a little extra time, exploring this area can be a great start to your river trip. Hiking on river left, across the river from the Lees Ferry ramp, offers you a chance to get away from the hustle and bustle of the put-in for some easy hiking. The ramp side of the river offers a few short easy hikes and a difficult one as well.

To go exploring on the river-left side of the Ferry, row across the river and head for the small fan of gravel coming into the river straight across from the boat launch. Tie up and work your way through the 100 feet of tamarisk onto the open plain just behind them. You are now on Navajo Nation land, and a permit is required to hike here. To the south, across the plain in front of you 100 yards or so, the remains of a small dugout cabin are visible. Halfway to this cabin, look for a barely discernible track winding its way to the west up the low rise of slickrock hills that make up Lee's Backbone.

If you follow this track west, look for petrified logs as soon as you start up the track. Another 1/3 mile along, the track has parallel wagon ruts cut into the Shinarump Conglomerate. Another 1/2 mile or so will take you past a large boulder, on which is inscribed the following: "DEC. 4 1878 THIS ROCK SENTINEL TO PASSING WAGONS OF FIRST MESA COMPANY ONDER THE COMAND OF HYRUM SMITH PHELPS." It doesn't take much of an imagination to see why this wagon road was called Lee's Backbone. Getting wagons and teams over this road must have been a real challenge.

If you walk to the north from this boulder back to the rim, you'll have a fine view of the Ferry and Lonely Dell across the river. If you hike back off the Backbone heading east, keep on the lookout for more petrified wood. The return route is the reverse of how you came. The route traverses a little over 2 miles round trip and can easily be covered in one to two hours.

If you are not up for rowing across the river, then an easy walk into the wash behind the restrooms at the boat ramp has some points of interest as well. From the boat ramp, cross the parking lot and walk into the dry wash behind the restrooms. One hundred yards or so from the parking lot there is a very nice petrified log in the bed of the wash. From here, hike up the slope to your left, which is creek right. This is a good introduction to creek right and left, terms you will need to understand well in this book.

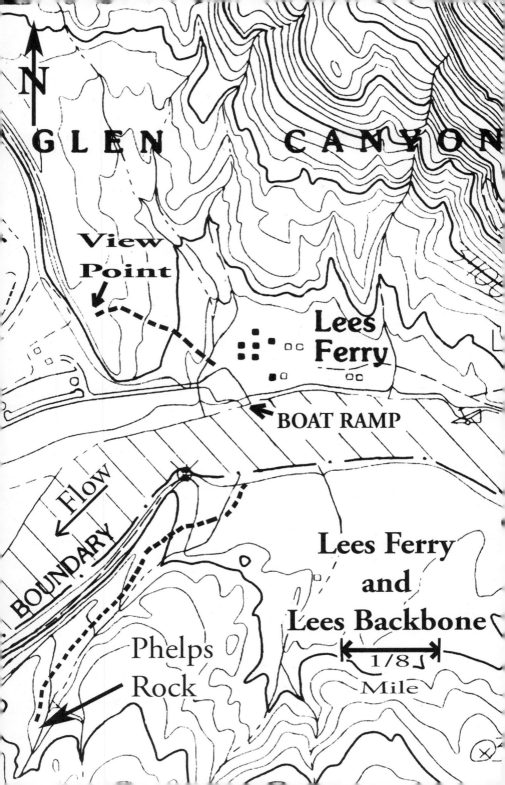

1. Lees Ferry, Lees Backbone and the Spencer Trail contd.

In less than 1/4 mile, you will reach the summit of a knoll with a small ancient Pueblo dwelling at its top. There is a fine view of the Lees Ferry Ranch from this point. The return is as you came.

For a more challenging hike with a fantastic view, you might want to walk up the 2-mile–long, difficult Spencer Trail. From the boat ramp, walk upstream through the dirt parking lot and along the riverside trail. In a little over 1/4 mile, look for the trail leaving the river and heading up a scree slope. This trail will switchback up to a cliff, then skirt to the north as it rises up through a break in the cliff face. After traversing less than1/2 mile, you will encounter another series of switchbacks. These will end in a short traverse back to the south. A final short series of switchbacks will take you to the top of the Navajo Sandstone ridgeline.

What a view! From here, directly to the east, is the Colorado River in the deeply entrenched Glen Canyon. Beyond that is Page, AZ and Lake Powell. Castle Rock is plainly visible 10 miles away to the northeast, with Navajo Mountain beyond that. To the southwest stretches the beginning of Grand Canyon National Park. You can clearly see the land rising up in the distance to the southwest. This view affords the hiker a clear picture of the river cutting into the rising Marble Platform and House Rock Valley, while forming the ever-deepening Marble Canyon. As the Colorado River heads south into Marble Canyon from Lee's Ferry to roughly the Nankoweap area, the land is rising up a little over 60 feet per mile. If you add this to the rivers down-cutting of 8 feet per mile, you can multiply the river mile X 70 to get a rough idea of the vertical rise from the river to the rim.

The return is as you came. Don't forget to bring your hat and a couple of quarts of water along for this hike during the summer months, and eat some salty snack foods along the way as well.

Lees Ferry
and the
Spencer Trail

1/4 Mile

2. Cathedral Wash

Though you aren't supposed to camp here if you are rafting Grand Canyon, there is a short hike out Cathedral Wash to the Lee's Ferry road. You can also hike in to the river from a small parking lot at the Lee's Ferry road, to watch river runners float by. The pull-in for Cathedral Wash is at Mile 2.75 R, just above the small riffle formed by the Cathedral Wash debris fan.

It's about a mile of easy walking up this tight twisting Kaibab Limestone drainage to the Lees Ferry road. There are a few pourovers you will need to scramble around. The biggest one is a 12-foot drop, and you can get around this on the creek-right side more easily than on creek left. If you are going to hike to the parking lot, you will need to stay in the left (or south) fork drainage once you have climbed up past this pourover. This is a wonderful half-day hike for visitors to the Lee's Ferry region, so you may run into hikers going to the river from the road.

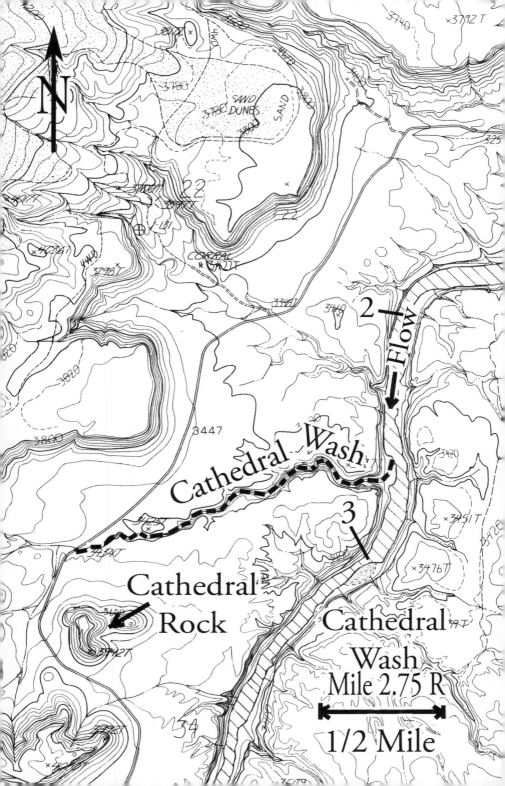

3. Jackass Creek

At the foot of Badger Rapid (Mile 8.0 L) is a great sandy camp with access to Jackass Creek. There's a fairly large eddy on this side of the river in the tail waves of Badger Rapid, so the pull-in is easy. If you find yourself here with some time for an easy hike, you are in luck. There are multiple routes to the rim up the creek.

As you leave the Colorado River and head up the creek, note the sheer cliff of Kaibab, Toroweap and Coconino formations. This 300-foot wall of rock layers is very common in the upper reaches of Marble Canyon in the side drainages. After roughly 1/3 mile, the creek narrows and you will come to a 40-foot pourover. There may be a rope hanging down from an anchor above. TEST this rope by pulling forcefully on it before you proceed if you are going to use it. Though not necessary, this rope provides a good aid for climbing over this pourover.

Once past this spot, the flat-bottomed creek proceeds another 1/3 mile or so to a fork. If you take the left or northern drainage, proceed another few hundred yards and look for a trail that climbs out the north side of the creek. It's only 1/4 mile or so up this route to the rim. At the rim you are entering the Navajo Nation. Looking east you can make out the buildings at Navajo Spring, a little over a mile away at highway 89 A. There are a few picnic benches here at the trailhead as well.

Meanwhile, if you decided to take the right or southern drainage at the fork, you can climb out here as well. Proceed on another 1/3 mile or so and look for a broken slope on the south side of the drainage. Don't worry if you can't find the "right" spot. You can continue on until you find a way up that looks like it will go. Chances are it will. After a short up-climb, you will top out on the Marble Platform. The vehicles that you hear are on nearby Highway 89A. Once at the rim, you are entering the Navajo Nation. I have not hiked beyond this point, but one day would like to hike due west from here the 3/4 mile to the rim. There should be a great view of camp and Badger Rapid awaiting those who check it out. The return is via your route up.

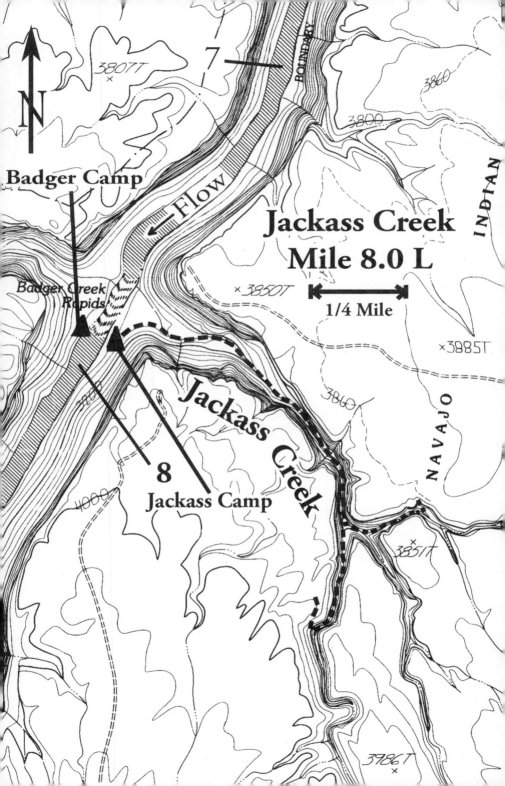

4. Soap Creek

Soap Creek offers some really fun hiking from a great river camp at Mile11.0 R. The camp is just above the rapid. If you are thinking to camp at the foot of Soap Creek on river right, best scout it out from the top first. The pull-in at the foot of the rapid is easy to miss. Soap Creek is an easy hike that will take you over a half-day to hike the four miles one way up to Highway 89A, very close to the Hatch River Expeditions warehouse at Cliff Dwellers, AZ.

From camp, proceed along the well-defined trail heading over to the bed of Soap Creek. As with all hikes in this book, hiking in riverbeds or on rock will always be the preferred route, while hiking over fragile desert soils off-trail is to be avoided at all cost. For the first mile, the riverbed is wide and easygoing, as you hike up through the Hermit Shale. At just over 11/2 miles from the river, you will pass a small seep. Depending on the time of year, you may find a few small pools of water here.

At this point, you will come to a fork in the canyon, with drainage's coming in on your right and left. Head left. In another 1/2 mile, you will hike up into the Coconino Sandstone. The canyon walls close in and you will need to start boulder-hopping. The boulders become living-room-sized at one point, and you will need to scout around for the best way to proceed up through this jumble of stone. You will need to scramble up a small pourover, then look for a small house-sized boulder you can walk/stoop under. Just past this boulder you will need to leave the creekbed and climb up the talus slope on creek right. Look for cairns making the trail here. Once you hike up this slope 100 feet or so, look for the trail heading level and back to the creek bed, past a 60-foot-high pourover.

From here, continue up the drainage floor another mile, then look for a small drainage coming in on your right. There are usually cairns here. Proceed up this smaller side tributary another 1/2 mile and you will come to the Soap Creek trailhead parking lot. From here you can walk along the road 1/2 mile to a small corral and line shack, then another 1/4 mile to Highway 89A. The Vermilion Cliffs are to your west and north, as they turn west and form the northern edge of the House Rock Valley. The Echo Cliffs are to the east, beyond the hidden Marble Canyon and your boats. To the south stretches the House Rock Valley. The return is as you have come. This is a hot hike in the middle of the summer, so bring some water and salty snack food. There will be ice in here in the winter.

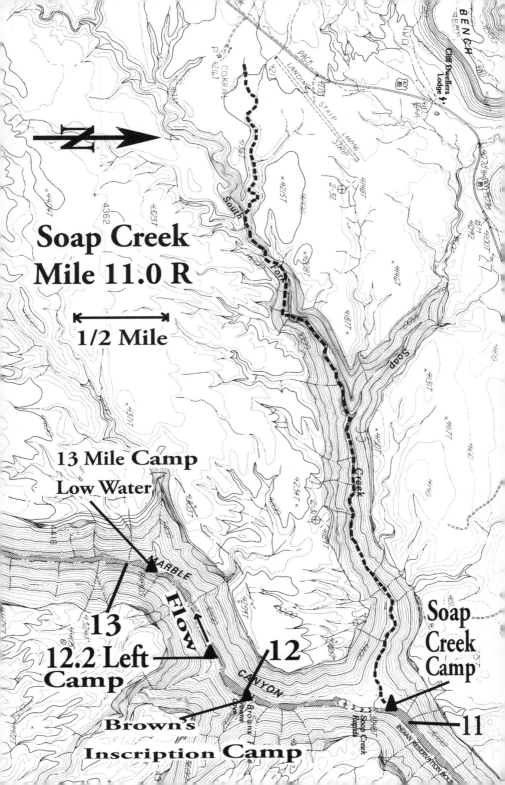

**Soap Creek
Mile 11.0 R**

1/2 Mile

13 Mile Camp
Low Water

13
12.2 Left
Camp

Flow

12

Brown's

Inscription Camp

Soap
Creek
Camp

11

5. Sheer Wall

Sheer Wall Rapid, at River Mile 14.2 L, is formed by the emergence of Tanner Wash coming in from the east. There are some wonderful Supai narrows at the mouth of Tanner, but the wash pours into the Colorado over a 30-foot waterfall, making access a challenge. There is usually a small trickle of water in the narrows from small seeps in the Supai.

There are a number of difficult ways to access Tanner Wash from the river. At Mile 14.0 L, look for an undercut bench with a small eddy just upstream from the bench. Park your boats in the eddy. You can camp on the bench if the dam is releasing less than 20 thousand cubic feet per second (cfs), with great early afternoon shade and late morning sun.

To begin your journey, either climb up the 30 feet of exposed crack at the eddy and set up a fixed rope for those who will need it, or walk around the bench downstream 100 yards or so to a small chimney with a 20-foot up-climb. From this point on either route, you will now be high enough to traverse downstream and up a bit on a fine Supai ledge. Follow the path here and don't step on the small cacti. The ledge pinches to a narrow point as it approaches the mouth of Tanner Wash, but you can find at least two narrow routes that allow you to proceed. There's a great bird's eye view down onto the mouth of the wash and Sheer Wall Rapid.

From this vantage point, you can continue into the Supai narrows of Tanner Wash. In less than 1/2 mile, the narrows end as you climb up into the Hermit Shale and a broad valley with cliffs on both rims. The route back to the boats from here is as you have come.

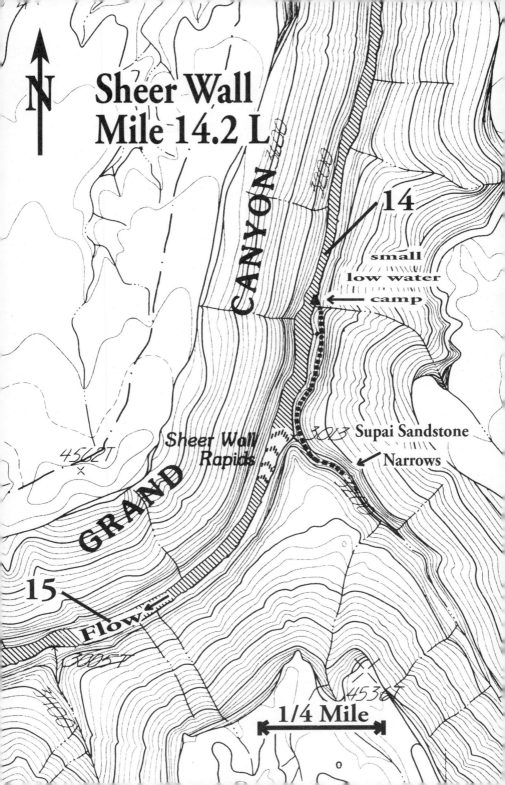

Sheer Wall
Mile 14.2 L

N

14

small
low water
← camp

Sheer Wall
Rapids

Supai Sandstone
Narrows

CANYON

GRAND

15

Flow

1/4 Mile

6. Rider Canyon

Most boaters are so focused on House Rock Rapid at Mile 16.9, few take the time to hike in Rider Canyon. There is a difficult hike of about 3 miles to the rim, along with some enjoyable and easy-to-access narrows close to the river. If House Rock Wash has recently flash-flooded, there may be some great mud in these narrows as well. Plan on a half day at least to rim out and return to the river.

To hike Rider Canyon, either tie up the boats at the top of House Rock Rapid, or run the rapid and catch the surging eddy at the foot of the rapid, both on river right. If Glen Canyon Dam is releasing over 20 thousand cfs, you may need to wade into or out of the mouth of Rider Canyon to begin or end your hike.

Once into the canyon, you will immediately enter some fine Supai narrows. There are a few pourovers to be scrambled around, but nothing of note to deal with. The narrows end and the canyon opens up into a sun-filled, boulder-strewn, tight wash. To continue your walk to the rim, you will need to hike up the wash bed another 2 miles. Rider Canyon bends from a westerly to a southwesterly trend after about a mile from the river. Continue another mile from this bend, and at this point look for a break on the southeast side of the canyon. There is a route leading up through a break in the solid Kaibab-Toroweap-Coconino walls here. In less than 1/2 mile you will be able to reach the rim. There is not much of a view from the rim, with few landmarks except for the Vermilion and Echo Cliffs to the north. From here, the adventurous hiker can walk overland 3/4 mile east-southeast to the Canyon rim, where a spectacular view of Boulder Narrows may be had.

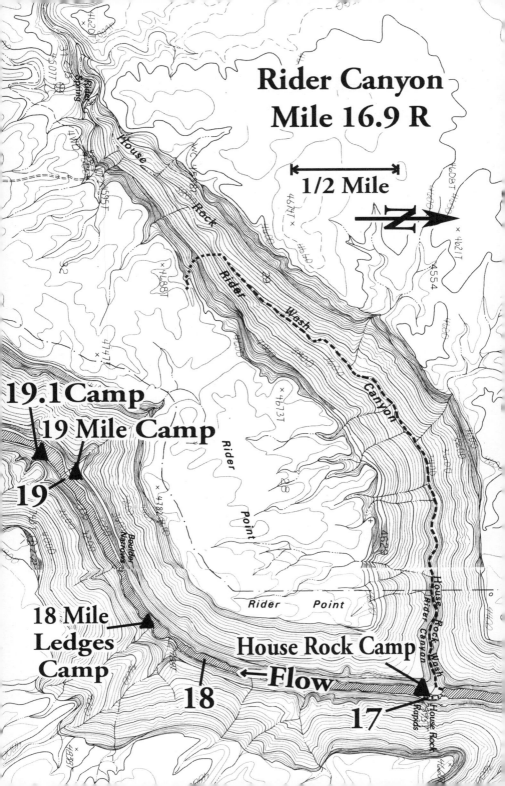

Rider Canyon
Mile 16.9 R

1/2 Mile

N

19.1 Camp

19 Mile Camp

19

18 Mile
Ledges
Camp

House Rock Camp

←Flow

18

17

7. 19 Mile Route

As the Colorado River begins to flow south into the uplift of the Marble Platform, routes to the rim become more infrequent. In the Marble Canyon area, one of the ways to climb to the rim is at 19 Mile on river right. This difficult route is only 1/2 mile but is very steep, with a lot of skill at route finding required.

The route starts at the bend in the river at Mile 19.0 R. Hike away from the river up the small boulder choked drainage you will find here. It's the only "easy" way through the solid Supai cliffs in this area. After 1/8 of a mile, start heading up to the west. There are some large boulders and broken cliffs to pick your way through about halfway to the rim. As you approach the Kaibab cliffs at the top, look for a chute that goes back to the north west. The route goes up this chute 100 yards or so to the rim.

Once you top out, there is an easy walk you might want to consider for a great view down on North Canyon Rapid. It's only 3/4 mile south along the rim to the overlook, and if you got this far, treat yourself to the view. Head south with the rim on your left. You will need to go up and down a few low hills to get to your destination, but keep going south. After a walk of a little over 1/2 mile, you will come to the corner of a cliff that defines the northern edge of North Canyon. The view down to the North Canyon Rapid is fantastic. Be careful at the edge here, especially on a windy day.

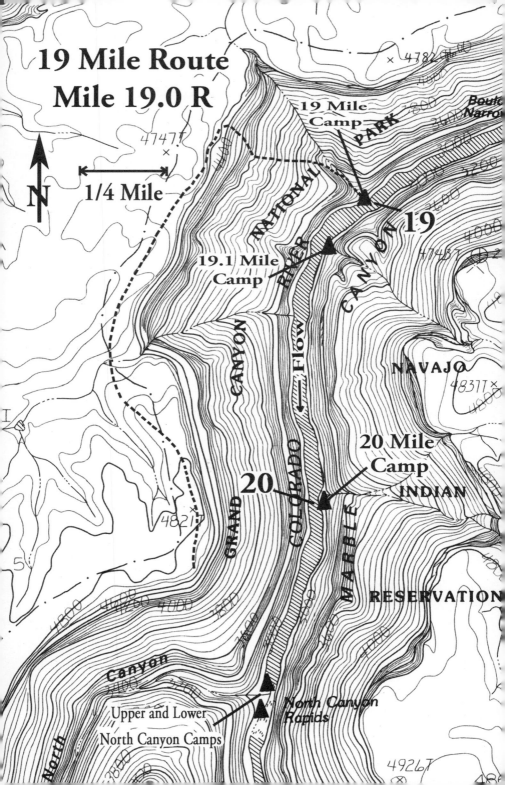

8. North Canyon

North Canyon is a popular easy side hike in upper Marble Canyon. North Canyon offers a short walk of 1/2 mile to summer shade, with a deep pool and occasional trickle of water, making this a wonderful spot indeed. There are two camps on river right at North Canyon (Mile 20.4 R), one just above the rapid, and the other at the rapid's foot. The upper camp has a large population of ants, and the lower camp has a surging eddy to park the boats. Otherwise, both are fine camps.

To hike the 1/2 mile to the deep pool, you will need to find a trail on the north side of the canyon (creek left), which starts at the canyon's mouth. You will walk past some impressively high, perched, flood-deposited mud banks from before the construction of Glen Canyon Dam. The trail goes up to a ledge, then there is a boost up a 5-foot-high pourover. From here you will need to climb up the trail 100 feet or more still on the north side of the canyon. Once you have made this climb, it's an easy walk along a bench into the canyon floor and shade.

Now that you are out of the sun, you'll come to the deep pool, which in wet years will have a small trickle of water coming down a flood-worn chute in the Supai Sandstone at the back of the pool. This pool can easily be 5 feet deep, and though agile climbers can try their luck climbing around the creek right side without falling in, most of us will need to get very wet if we want to reach the chute on the far side and continue our exploration.

With a little work the chute on the far side can be climbed, and the route now continues up the south side of the canyon. You'll need to climb up 60 or so feet on this side of the canyon using some natural sandstone steps. From here, walk back into the canyon bed. With a little scrambling, one will reach the end of the line at an over 40-foot-high pourover. Most folks stop here, hang out, and then head back to the Colorado following the trail they came up.

The adventurous and foolhardy may want to attempt the very difficult fault route out the north side of the Supai cliffs. Be forewarned: there is a lot of exposure on this route, with at least one point requiring the navigation of a cliff edge without protection. To attempt this route, you will need to retrace your steps to just about the point where you need to move to creek right and traverse to the 60 feet of sandstone steps. You'll want to look for a small fracture system that goes up and a bit downstream in the creek left wall. This is the route up and out. Again, it is not easy and requires a climb of well over 100 feet up an exposed cliff.

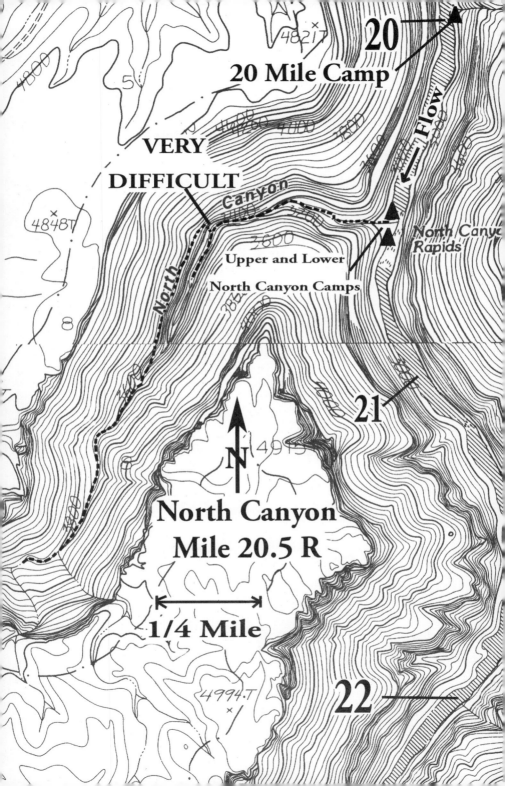

20

20 Mile Camp

Flow

VERY

DIFFICULT

Canyon

North

North Canyon
Rapids

Upper and Lower

North Canyon Camps

21

N

**North Canyon
Mile 20.5 R**

|← 1/4 Mile →|

1/4 Mile

22

8. North Canyon contd.

Once at the top of the fracture system, walk southwest along some sheer ledges and back into the canyon floor. As you make your traverse along these ledges, be very careful not to let loose any rocks that could hit fellow canyon visitors below you. Once you reach the creekbed, it's a fairly easy walk up the drainage through the Toroweap formation. This is as far as this writer made it before impending darkness forced a retreat. There is no water up here and little shade on a sunny day. As with all side canyons, summer monsoons may cause unexpected flash-flooding. If you are caught above the swimming pool during a flash-flood, you may have to wait many hours before the flood subsides.

Red ants often overrun the heavily used upper North Canyon camp. Boy, does their bite pack a punch. Those ants are living on river runners who leave them the inadvertent crumb and the odd bit of micro-trash. The better we keep our camp clean, the higher the chances that the ants will need to forage for food away from camp.

9. Lone Cedar and 24.5 Mile

Just below 23 Mile Rapid (Mile 23.25) is an amazing tree that you ought to stop and check out if you get a chance. After looking at the tree and running 24 Mile Rapid, if your party is ready to camp at 24.5 Mile Rapid, there is a great little hike you can do from there.

On a hot July 13, 1889, the Denver, Colorado Canyon and Pacific Railroad survey party, led by Robert Brewster Stanton, had lunch in the shade of a Utah juniper at the back of a small eddy (Mile 23.5) on river left. This eddy is just below the foot of 23 Mile Rapid. One of the survey crew, Harry McDonald, carved his initials on the side of this tree. "H McD" is what he carved. This "Lone Cedar" is still alive and well today. This tree is historic, so please do not disturb it.

To look at this inscription, you will need to run 23 Mile Rapid and the next riffle below it. There is a pourover on river left in this riffle, and you will need to be ready to row hard to the left shore just below this rock. As soon as you are below the rock, you will see a medium-sized eddy with a lot of driftwood on the sandy shore. Up above the old high water line stands a lone juniper tree. There is a lot of current moving past this eddy, so be ready to pull hard if you want to make it in. If you don't make the eddy, you can eddy out downstream and hike back up. From the beach, follow the path up through the perched old high water driftwood to the tree. Please don't wander off the path here, as the cryptobiotic soil is easily destroyed if you walk on it. Return the way you came.

Meanwhile, downstream on river left, at the top of 24.5 Mile Rapid, there is a nice camp, with good afternoon sun on a winter trip and late morning shade in the summer and a fun little hike in the wash behind camp. The hike is less than a mile, and gets you up to a fine view of the stretch of river you are boating through.

From camp, hike south over the debris fan formed by Sheep Spring Wash to the wash itself. There's a good scout of 24.5 Mile Rapid here. After you've looked at the rapid, walk up the steeply climbing wash a little over 1/4 mile to the first major fork. Turn left and climb up the very steep angle-of-repose boulder pile on this arm of the wash. You will top out on a flat bench at the top of the Supai. Walk back west on the flat bench a few hundred yards to the edge of the bench. Camp is just below you, as is another view of 24.5 Mile Rapid. 24 Mile Rapid is just upstream to the north, as are the two Supai towers in this section, the one on river right by 23 Mile Rapid, and the other one closer to you on river left. 25Mile Rapid is visible to the south. Return the way you came for a good two-hour stroll.

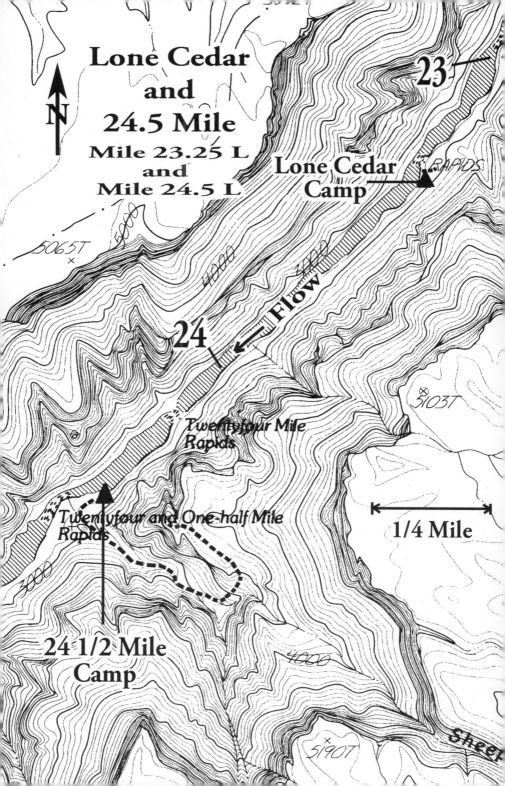

Lone Cedar
and
24.5 Mile
Mile 23.25 L
and
Mile 24.5 L

N

23

Lone Cedar
Camp

RAPIDS

5065T

4000

3000

Flow

24

5103T

Twentyfour Mile
Rapids

1/4 Mile

Twentyfour and One-half Mile
Rapids

3000

24 1/2 Mile
Camp

4000

5190T

Sheet

10. Silver Grotto

There is a nice camp at the eddy just below the rapid at Shinumo Wash (Mile 29.25 L). This camp offers early shade and late morning sun, plus difficult access to a wonderful limestone slot canyon called Silver Grotto. Its nickname, "Shiver Grotto," is indicative of the fact that access to the grotto is through 1/4 mile's worth of pools full of water that are too deep to wade. Being wet in the shade is a fast way to hypothermia on anything but the hottest of summer days.

To access the grotto, hike the few hundred feet to the mouth of Shinumo Wash. Good scramblers can manage the slick climb up the smooth limestone tongue after swimming the often 8 foot-deep plunge pool at the tongue's base. There are two alternate routes around this tongue, creek right or left. Both are exposed and can only be negotiated by those who are surefooted and willing to tempt the fates.

Once at the top of the tongue, there is a chock boulder where a throw bag may be anchored and let down to help others climb the tongue. From here it's a wade/swim through three more pools and two more slick steep water slides before one finally reaches the grotto. There is a fine limestone plunge pool at the base of one last 15-foot climb for those with a will to try. Once above this point, further progress is terminated by a 50-foot waterfall. There are some weeping springs here in the limestone. The climb down from this point is fun, as either you make it or you fall off the rock into a deep pool of water. Visiting Silver Grotto requires teamwork. Help each other when the going gets difficult, and plan your visit around lunchtime or early afternoon to benefit from the heat of the day. This is not a safe place to visit in monsoon season.

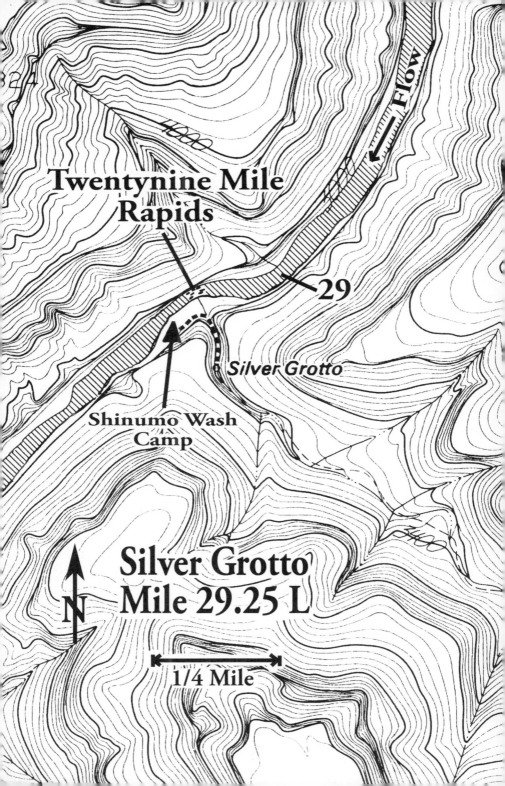

Flow

Twentynine Mile
Rapids

29

Silver Grotto

Shinumo Wash
Camp

N

Silver Grotto
Mile 29.25 L

1/4 Mile

11. Fence Fault and Shinumo Wash

In the late 1940s, the search for dam sites in Marble Canyon focused on the Redwall Cavern and Marble Canyon locations. Access to the Redwall Cavern dam site was via a pack trail constructed down Shinumo Wash, also known as 29 Mile Canyon. You can follow this easy trail all the way out to the rim, and though washed out in spots, the "trail" is still a great walk. A good way to stage for this hike is to camp at any camp between North Canyon and Shinumo Wash (the closer the better). Pack a lunch after you eat breakfast, then row the "Roaring Twenties" to the pull-in. From here you can hike all day and then look for camp downriver, the first of which is at Mile 30.4 R, just across the river. You can't easily row to this camp from the lower pull-in mentioned in the next two paragraphs due to the strong current and close proximity of this camp. Don't worry if you miss it--the next camp (also on river right) is just around the next riffle 1/4 mile downriver, at Mile 30.5 R.

The pull-in for this hike can be made at either of two points. The upper one requires you to pull in on river left at the foot of the small riffle at Mile 30.3 L. Stay close to the left side of the riffle and pull on in to the small eddy at the foot of this riffle. There is a nice sandy beach here. The downside to this pull-in is that you will have to negotiate a small section of Redwall cliff to start this hike from here. Look for a way up on the creek left side of the small side canyon that forms the boulder pile you are standing on. Once on top of the Redwall, walk downriver a few hundred yards and then climb up to the small saddle directly above you. Don't cut back to the right and walk downriver, as that path leads off to the Redwall Cavern Dam site (hike #12), which is another hike altogether.

The lower pull-in is just 100 yards or less below this riffle on river left, where the Redwall cliff breaks up and a talus slope reaches down to the river. There is no sandy beach here at this small pull-in. If the river is down, you may notice water bubbling up through the broken rock at your pull-in. This is part of the Fence Fault spring complex. After tying up, you will need to walk up the small draw above you, joining the small track that the folks who parked upstream will use, except you will have avoided the Redwall cliff they climbed through. Again, hike up to the saddle.

From the top of this saddle, hike northeast down the other side of the ridge you have just climbed, into a small drainage. Climb up out of the small drainage on the other side, and continue contouring at this same level, still going northeast.

25

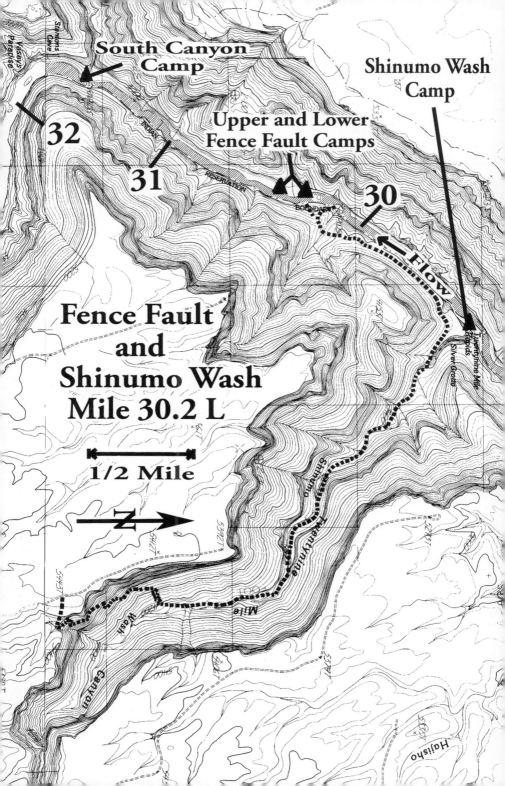

South Canyon
Camp

Shinumo Wash
Camp

Upper and Lower
Fence Fault Camps

32

31

30

Flow

Fence Fault
and
Shinumo Wash
Mile 30.2 L

1/2 Mile

N

11. Fence Fault and Shinumo Wash contd.

Continue hiking close to the top of the Redwall. A short side excursion to the edge gives you an impressive view of the Colorado River 300 feet below.

About 3/4 mile from the boats the trail curves to the southeast and parallels the top of the deep Redwall narrows of Silver Grotto (hike #10). You might want to walk over to the edge here as well and take a look down into this Redwall slot canyon. Please don't throw rocks over the edge here (or anywhere). Another 1/4 mile or so and you will meet up with the bed of Shinumo Wash.

From here, the trail proceeds to cross and re-cross the wash as it winds its way southeasterly for another 2.5 miles or so in the wide-open 29 Mile Canyon. At this point, the trail makes the final wash-crossing to the south side of the canyon and climbs steeply up the slope to the base of the Coconino. A short section of rockwork and dynamited shelf gets you through a small section of Coconino cliff, then the trail switchbacks the last 1/2 mile or so to the rim, at which point you enter the Navajo Nation. I was too tired and it was too late in the day for more exploring, but it's only 1.5 miles overland west-northwest to the rim, and I bet there's a great view of the Canyon from there. If you attempt such a walk, be sure to take a lot of mental notes on how to find your way back over the flat tableland of the rim to the trailhead. It would be most unfortunate to be unable to locate the tip-off point for the return walk down-trail. The trail back to the boats is the same as the one that got you here.

12. Fence Fault to Redwall Cavern Dam Site

In the late 1940s, the search for dam sites in Marble Canyon focused on the Redwall Cavern and Marble Canyon locations. Access to the Redwall Cavern dam site was via a pack trail constructed down Shinumo Wash. Once reaching the river, the trail went 3 miles downriver on top of the Redwall to the dam site above Redwall Cavern. Though washed out in spots, the "trail" is still a great easy walk.

The pull-ins for this hike are the same as for hike # 11. Everything is the same, except the route you take from the small saddle. Don't cut back to the left and walk upriver, as that path leads off to the Silver Grotto overlook and the route to the rim, which is hike #11.

From the saddle, hike up the ridge leading downstream, looking for a path down-canyon to your right. This trail was built for stock, and on the sections that are not washed out, is still in good shape. If you find yourself way up in the Supai and off-route, well, you're off-route. Hike back down closer to the Redwall edge and keep looking for the trail. Walking 2 miles downriver will take you to the top of the Redwall across from South Canyon. With Stanton's Cave in sight, you will find a small platform with a few bits of tent from a small camp. A little farther along, Vasey's Paradise comes into fine view, as does Redwall Cavern itself. You can follow this trail another mile to the dam site camp. Not much of interest there, but the anchor for the tramway to the rim has a little note left in the cement poured in 1951.

It will take the better part of a cool day to explore this area well, and on a hot summer day, you don't even want to think about this hike, as there is no water and no shade.

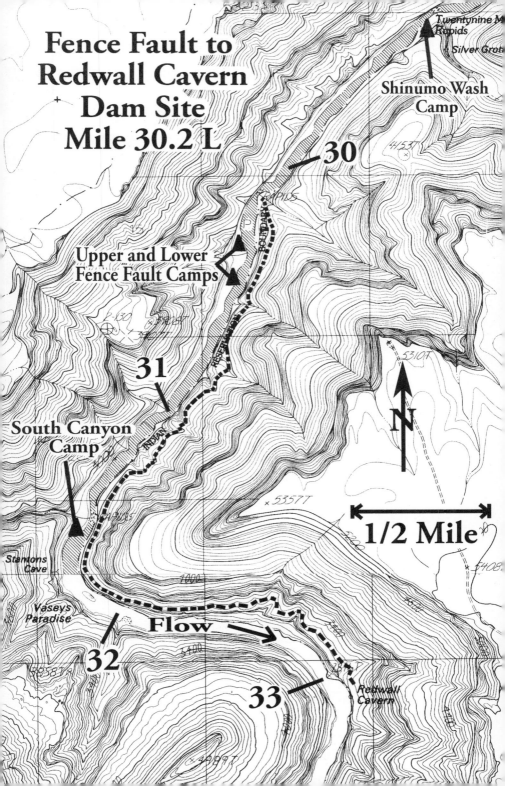

Fence Fault to Redwall Cavern Dam Site Mile 30.2 L

Twentynine M Rapids

Silver Groto

Shinumo Wash Camp

30

Upper and Lower Fence Fault Camps

BOUNDARY

RESERVATION

31

INDIAN

South Canyon Camp

N

× 5357 F

1/2 Mile

Stantons Cave

Vaseys Paradise

Flow

32

33

Redwall Cavern

13. Fence Fault to the West

The Fence Fault camp at River Mile 30.4 R, and the Lower Fence Fault camp, at Mile 30.5 R, are the camps of choice for an easy hike to the top of the Redwall or a more challenging hike up the Fence Fault to the rim. This difficult but direct hike is best done from a layover at either camp. The Lower Fence Fault camp is on a sandbar which is getting smaller by the year, so if the upper camp is open, camp there. You can miss the Fence Fault camp pull-in, so be ready to pull toward the river right shore as soon as you run the small riffle at 30.3. There's an eddy on the right, and the camp is just below this eddy. The hike to the rim will be a short hike, of under 4 miles, but will require boulder hopping, talus slope scrambling, and an elevation gain of 2,400 feet to the rim. To hike from the lower camp, you will need to proceed upriver toward the upper camp 100 yards or so past broken Redwall cliffs, into a small drainage that makes the Fence Fault debris fan. From the upper camp, you will need to hike 100 yards downriver to this same small drainage. The route up through the Redwall is just downstream of this drainage, up the ridge on the south side of the drainage.

For those who would like to attempt the journey to the rim, you will need to proceed downriver along the top of the Redwall a little over 1/4 mile. You will then see a fault-formed chute going up into the Supai and twisting to the west. To proceed up this chute you will need to do a lot of boulder hopping. There is one slightly exposed traverse near the very top of the chute. If you attempt to climb out through the Supai in the drainage that makes the Fence Fault debris fan, and are a very good climber, it "can" be done, but is beyond the "very difficult" scale in this book. Once you have cleared the chute and are on top of the Supai, there is a very fine view of this region if you hike out to the point just east of the top of the chute. There's a view of South Canyon to the south, and the river above Fence Fault to the north. This view is worth the diversion. From here, hike to a 30-foot-high "Hoodoo" of Kaibab limestone on top of a pillar of Hermit Shale toward the drainage to the west. Stay at this level, cross the drainage and proceed south to the base of the scree slope that extends all the way up through the broken Coconino Sandstone. You will need to skirt a debris cliff before going up the scree slope. Once you top the Coconino, the route proceeds north and then west along the base of broken Kaibab cliffs. There are multiple routes up through the broken Kaibab at the Fence Fault to the rim that require a little scrambling. To take in the full view, hike up the Kaibab cliffs to the north. From this prominence, you can see the Fence Fault Camp at your feet, Marble Canyon twisting to the south, Shinumo Altar to the east, and the Echo Cliffs to the north. The route down is as you have come. Bring food, water and a hat. Don't think about this hike in the hottest of summer days.

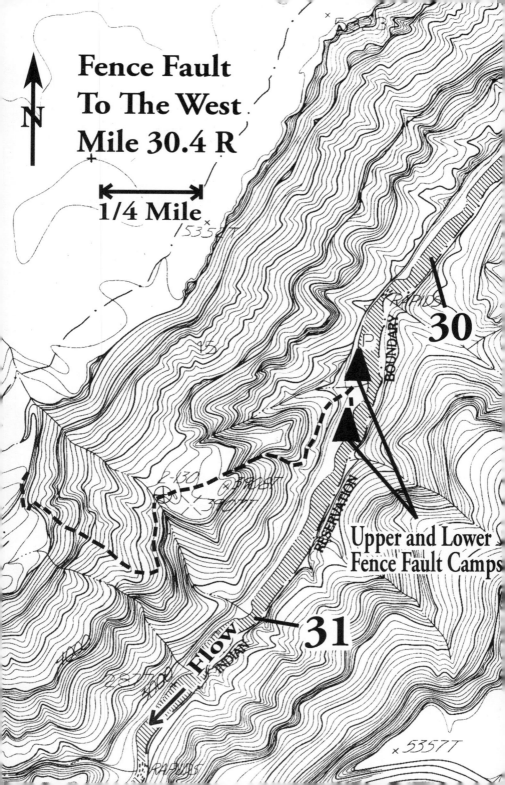

Fence Fault
To The West
Mile 30.4 R

N

1/4 Mile

30

Upper and Lower
Fence Fault Camps

31

14. South Canyon, Stanton's Cave and Bedrock Canyon

There's a lot to do here at South Canyon, from an easy exploration of Stanton's Cave and the ancient Pueblo dwellings just above camp, to the difficult hike out the corner pocket route up South Canyon. The camp here (Mile 31.6 R), at the top of the large South Canyon eddy, is highly used, and you may share your camp with backpackers who have hiked in from South Canyon.

To hike to Stanton's Cave, you will need to climb to the top of the Redwall cliff that is the back wall of your kitchen and just 60 feet high. There are a number of ways up through this cliff; the easiest is behind camp (upriver) up the sand dune. Look for a route in a small recess in the cliff. If you have passed the mouth of South Canyon, you've walked too far. Once on top of the Redwall, walk downriver and you will find a trail heading up as it goes along. In about 1/4 mile you will be at the base of the Redwall and heading straight into the mouth of Stanton's Cave.

The foolhardy may try to walk on around to Vasey's Paradise. It's easy going till the very end, when the slick Muav Limestone gets very steep, and a slip will send you into the fast current of the cold Colorado below. If you make it across this section, you will find yourself in the vegetation at Vasey's Paradise. Congratulations. You have just entered one of three locations in the Canyon that have poison ivy. That nice green leafy stuff you are standing in. You got it. The best way to get to Vasey's is by water.

To see some 900-year-old ancestral Puebloan dwellings, hike upriver out of camp, pass the mouth of South Canyon and proceed upriver to the first small beach you encounter. You may have to wade along shore if the Colorado is up. At the back of this small beach is a break in an extension of the same 60-foot- high limestone cliff you hiked through to go to Stanton's Cave. Climb up this break to the cliff top. There are dwellings and a few petroglyphs just downriver. Please stay on the path here and avoid walking off the trail.

If you want to attempt the difficult 1/4 mile climb to the top of the Redwall, look for a trail that goes upriver from the petroglyphs and climbs quickly to the base of the massive Redwall cliffs. The trail goes up over a point of Redwall with some exposure, then ascends a small draw to the top of the Redwall. Follow the trail back downriver along the top of the Redwall, and where the trail turns west into the South Canyon drainage, go over to the Redwall edge for a fine view of the river. Use caution at the edge. Do not step on desert plants.

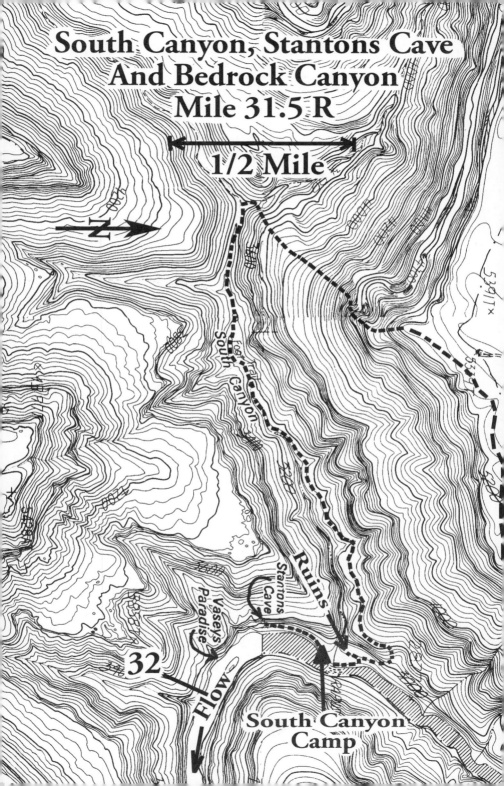

South Canyon, Stantons Cave
And Bedrock Canyon
Mile 31.5 R

1/2 Mile

South Canyon

Ruins

Stantons Cave

Vasey's Paradise

32

Flow

South Canyon
Camp

14. South Canyon, Stanton's Cave and Bedrock Canyon contd.

If you have the time, it's possible to rim out from here. It is best to lay over for this difficult hike. Once you have come up through the Redwall, stay on this trail. You will cross and re-cross the South Canyon Wash, hiking up-canyon about 1.25 miles or so. A large canyon will enter from the north. This is Bedrock Canyon. From here, you will need to leave the main trail and hike up the steep ridge at the east corner of Bedrock and South Canyons for a little over 1/2 mile. Follow the route up through the broken Coconino and Toroweap, through the Kaibab cliffs and to the rim. From here, it's only 3/4 of a mile east to another location on the rim with a very fine view of the Canyon. The way back to the boats is as you came. This hike takes well over a half-day up and back, and should not be done in the summer heat. Bring lots of water and snack foods on this hike.

---

15. Nautiloid Canyon

There is a nice camp a few miles below the South Canyon and Redwall Cavern areas, with a great easy walk from camp into a small drainage with some wonderful chambered nautiloid fossils. The camp (Mile 34.75 L) is on the left at the foot of the eddy formed by a small riffle at River Mile 34.75. Hike 100 yards into the drainage just upstream from camp. You will need to negotiate about 75 feet of broken limestone cliff, which you can climb either on creek right in the drainage or just upriver another 100 yards or so. Either way leads right back into the drainage above the cliffs.

From here, proceed only 50 yards or so into the drainage. The fossils you are looking for are on the bare limestone floor of the drainage. It helps to see their outlines if you pour a little water on them. There is great shade here at noon on a hot summer day. Return by your route up. This is a main attraction site and you may find other river parties stopping to look at these wonderful fossils with your group. It's a great opportunity to make new river friends and ask that all important question, "Hey, where are you camping tonight?"

Little Redwall
Camp

Nautiloid
Canyon
Mile 34.75 L

34

Flow →

Hanging
Springs

Nautiloid
Camp

35

N

1/4 Mile

16. Brower's Bower

Just above the Marble Canyon dam site at Mile 39.5 is a wonderful small camp and short easy hike into a small side canyon, recently nicknamed "Brower's Bower." David Brower is credited more then anyone else for the halting of dam construction at this location. The pull-in is on river right at Mile 39.0 at the foot of a small riffle. If you are headed for any of the river camps between Buck Farm and the top of President Harding Rapid in the wintertime when fires are permitted in fire pans, you may want to stop and look for firewood on the beach here.

To hike to Brower's Bower, look for a small trail winding into the downstream (south) side of the small canyon coming through the towering Redwall Limestone cliffs found here. You won't get far up this drainage, but if it's late March or early April, the redbuds should be in bloom. This canyon is prone to flash floods in monsoon season, so the redbuds are occasionally beat down by the flood waters. If you find yourself here in deep shade on a hot summer day, think of Dave for a moment. Imagine yourself under a few hundred feet of water. Then thank Dave for all you see. Please don't wander off-trail here. Every grain of fragile desert soil is singing Dave's praise here too.

Brower's Bower
Low-Water Camp

39

Brower's Bower
Mile 39.0 R

M
A
R
B
L
E

C
A
N
Y
O
N

4400

4200

Marble Canyon
Dam Site

3630AT

40

3800

Flow

4000

3800

N

1/4 Mile

17. Buck Farm Canyon

Buck Farm Canyon is a tight Redwall Canyon with a great camp at its mouth. This is not a hike with a view of a lot of country, but offers a great 1/2 mile to a mile easy walk into some shade with permanent water. You can easily spend a few hours here. The pull-in for the camp is at the top of the riffle and halfway around the debris fan at Mile 41.0 R. There is another pull-in at the very top of the debris fan if you are just stopping to hike. There is some winter sun, and afternoon shade in the summer.

To hike Buck Farm, grab a water bottle and some snack food before you hike along the trail over the sand dune behind camp and into the wash coming out of the Canyon. That black-looking stuff on the ground everywhere off the trail is indeed alive. It's the microbiotic crust mentioned in the introduction. This living plant is counting on you not to step on it. There is a little rock scrambling at the mouth, as you walk under a hanging boulder in the middle of the drainage. Continue on another 1/4 mile or so, passing around a few small pourovers. The creekbed narrows at this point, and you have two options. Either head out of the creekbed on creek left up a hundred feet or so into a small bowl and traverse 1/4 mile back into the drainage. This is the easy route. Your other option is to stay low and work your way through the narrows. If you stay in the narrows, you will have to get around an impressive pourover by climbing in some exposed cliffs on creek left.

Either route will lead you back to another pourover in less than 1/4 mile. Look for a route around this spot on creek right. From here there are a few more easily passed chockstones to the final bowl that turns most folk back. At this point you are almost a mile from the river, and in the deep recesses of a tight Redwall Canyon. The redbud trees, cattails and cottonwoods make this a very enjoyable hike most of the year. You may find other river parties stopped here. This is a good time to discuss your future travel plans with other river parties before you reach the Nankoweap area. This is also a highly used camp. Try to leave this and all your camps cleaner than when you arrived.

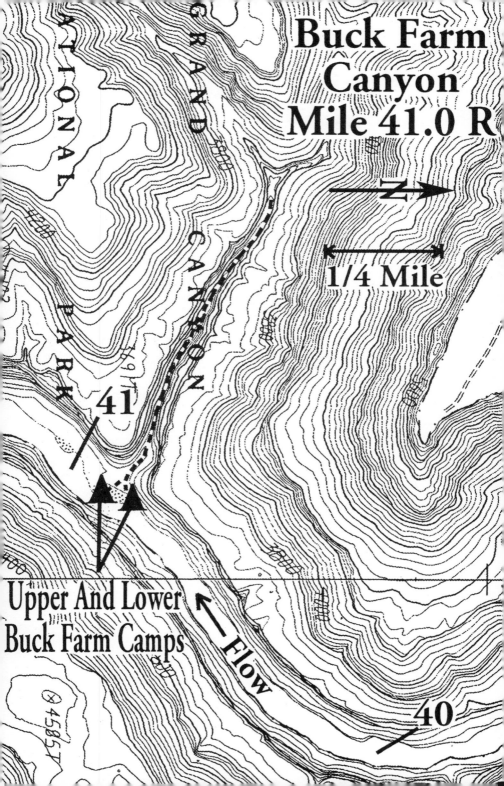

Buck Farm
Canyon
Mile 41.0 R

1/4 Mile

41

40

Upper And Lower
Buck Farm Camps

Flow

18. Bert's Boat and Bert's Canyon

There is a wonderful shady little canyon with a trickle of water in a small green chasm that is named for the Grand Old Man of the River, Bert Loper. Bert was presumed to have had a heart attack while rowing 24.5 Mile Rapid on a hot July day in 1949, at the ripe old age of 79. Bert's boat was found just above the canyon that bears his name, and was pulled up above high water and left. Some pieces of plywood are all that remain from the day in 1949 when his boat was laid to rest here.

The pull-in for this short easy hike is just above the debris fan made by Bert's Canyon (Mile 41.3 R). From here there is a small path behind the thick riverside vegetation at the base of the scree slope leading downstream toward the mouth of Bert's Canyon. Just before you reach the debris fan at the mouth of Bert's Canyon, look for the plywood outline of a boat below a large mesquite tree. There is not a lot left of Bert's boat, so take only pictures, and please leave what little remains of Bert's boat.

You can continue on another 1/4 mile or less along this path as it winds its way into Bert's Canyon. The old tables you will find are from the 1940s dam-building days. The path ends at the base of a small waterfall with a few redbud trees. The shade in here is wonderful on a hot summer day. The walk back to the boats, 1/4 mile or so, is as you came.

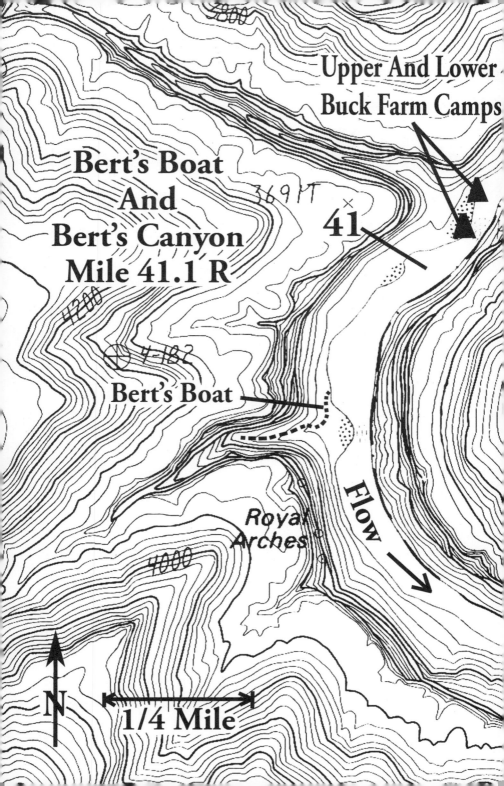

Upper And Lower
Buck Farm Camps

Bert's Boat
And
Bert's Canyon
Mile 41.1 R

41

3691T

4200

4182

Bert's Boat

Royal
Arches

Flow

4000

N

1/4 Mile

19. Eminence Break

The Eminence Break Fault is a major fault system that intersects the Colorado River in a number of places. Not far below President Harding Rapid there is a great camp, from which you can hike the difficult route to the top of the Redwall on river left, and on to the rim if you are so inclined. Ideally you would like to camp at the start of this route, at the camp just below the small dog-leg riffle at Mile 44.6 L. The route starts just upstream from camp. Yes, it is steep. Follow the cairned route up through the Redwall. There is some multiple trailing in spots, so try to come down the way you got up. Once up to the top of the Redwall, you will find a fine view of President Harding Rapid below and Saddle Mountain to the west.

Depending on how hot it is and how much time you have, for those who found the climb up through the Redwall easy, the route continues northeast and along the fault into the corner pocket drainage. Don't turn east up the good-sized drainage coming in from that direction. Cross it and continue northeast. Again, this route has some multiple trailing as it finds its way up VERY steep slopes of broken Supai through the Coconino and finally into Kaibab Limestone at the rim. Just before the top, the route goes under a large Kaibab boulder.

Once at the top, Shinumo Altar is to your east, the Vermilion Cliffs and Lee's Ferry are to your north, Saddle Mountain and the East Kaibab Monocline rise up in a thousand feet of gently elevated terrain to your west, and there is a fantastic view of Point Hansbrough below you. The view south is obscured by the low hills of Cedar Ridge. If you attempt to rim out here, carry at least 3 quarts of water and, some sort of carbos and electrolytes. Take your time, and plan on taking the day to do this hike justice.

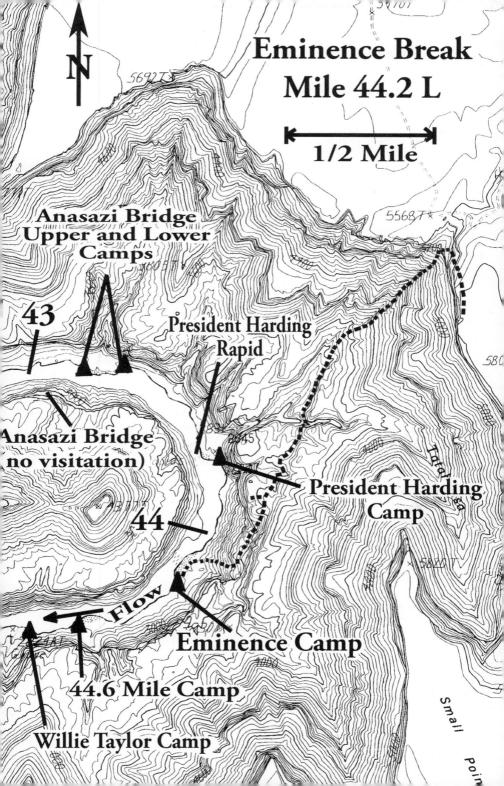

Eminence Break
Mile 44.2 L

N

1/2 Mile

Anasazi Bridge
Upper and Lower
Camps

43

President Harding
Rapid

Anasazi Bridge
(no visitation)

44

President Harding
Camp

Flow

Eminence Camp

44.6 Mile Camp

Willie Taylor Camp

20. Saddle Canyon

There are two camps that offer easy access to the shade and peaceful waterfall at Saddle Canyon (Mile 47.0 R). The upper camp has two pull-ins and can serve as two camps. The upper pull-in is right at the point where the Saddle Canyon debris fan meets the eddy just below the fan. The lower pull-in for this same camp is right around the corner, but against the eddy current. It's a lot easier to float out in the eddy and ride the current back to the pull-in. The other camp is across the eddy and downstream, at the point where the current goes either into the eddy or on downriver. This is another heavily used river camp. You will do all river runners a service by leaving this camp cleaner than you found it.

From either camp, you will need to walk the trail to the base of the slope to the west and follow the well-used path to a steep chute with a trail going up it. At the top of this chute, the trail levels out and heads around the hillside and up into a canyon filled with hackberry and ash trees. Continue on the path into the Saddle Canyon narrows. There is a chockstone just below the final pool and waterfall, where some folks may require a boost. There is shade on a hot sunny day here. This is a heavily visited attraction site in the summer, and you may have to share your time here with others. The way back to the camps is by the same mile-long route you took to get here.

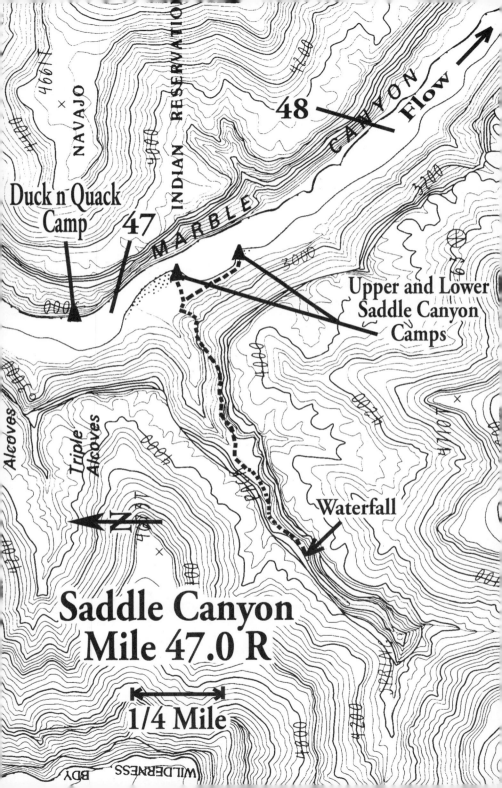

21. Little Nankoweap Creek to Boundary Ridge

There are four great camps in the Nankoweap area, all of which provide access to this wonderful area. The first camp is just above the mouth of Little Nankoweap (Mile 51.75 R). This camp has a high sandbank to climb from the boats to the camp, but allows access to the entire Nankoweap area. The other 3 camps are below the main Nankoweap Rapid: the first is at the cobble eddy at the foot of the rapid, at Mile 52.6 R; the second is at the big eddy below that, at Mile 53.0 R; and the third is at the point just below the big eddy, at Mile 53.2 R. This is a highly used area, and you can expect to share access to the many attractions here with other river runners. The Little Nankoweap drainage offers an easy hike of a little over a mile into some deep shade, or a very difficult hike on up through the Redwall and to the rim at the eastern edge of Boundary Ridge, for the ambitious ones in your group.

The best camp for these hikes is from the upper camp at Mile 51.75 R, but by hiking upriver along the trail system from the three lower camps, you can reach the Little Nankoweap drainage as well. Once in the drainage, hike up the dry wash bed 3/4 mile to a fork in the canyon. You can proceed up the western arm another 1/4 mile or so into some wonderful limestone narrows with a dry waterfall at the end. There is no water here, but in the hot summer, there will be shade. From this fork, you can also take the north arm, and hike right through the Redwall.

If you want to try the very difficult Redwall route, proceed 1/4 mile or less up the north arm, and look for a small path that climbs the east side of the drainage to pass a boulder-choked section of the drainage. This path drops back into the drainage, which is by this time getting very constricted. The key here is to cross to the west side of the drainage at this point, and hike up a small talus slope away from the drainage a few hundred yards. A broken chute will present itself, and you will need to climb up that chute. Proceed north up a broken ridge, and within just over 1/4 mile from the fork, you will reach the top of the Redwall.

If you want to reach Boundary Ridge from here, follow the drainage north-northeast, up a small chute in the Supai above you. It's less than 1/4 mile, but requires a steep uphill climb. At the top of this chute you will crest a ridge. From here, hike this ridge up and to the northwest, through the Supai and into the Coconino. Avoid trampling the fragile desert soils here. Pick your way up the ridge, passing through the Coconino, and into the Toroweap-Kaibab. There is a south-facing chute at the top of this ridge that goes to the rim. You will have to do a

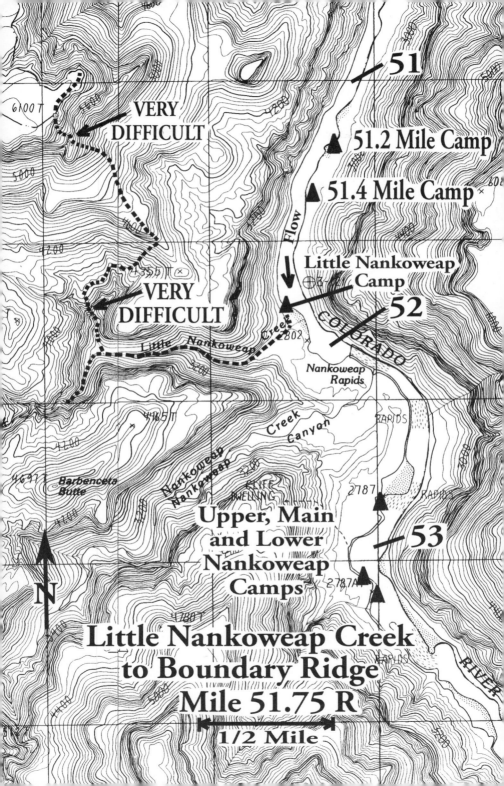

51

51.2 Mile Camp

51.4 Mile Camp

Flow

VERY DIFFICULT

Little Nankoweap Camp

52

VERY DIFFICULT

Little Nankoweap Creek

COLORADO

Nankoweap Rapids

Barbenceta Butte

RAPIDS

Nankoweap Creek Canyon

Nankoweap

CLIFF DWELLING

2787

RAPIDS

Upper, Main and Lower Nankoweap Camps

53

2787A

N

RIVER

Little Nankoweap Creek to Boundary Ridge
Mile 51.75 R

1/2 Mile

21. Little Nankoweap Creek to Boundary Ridge contd.

little traversing to get into this chute, and there are a few ledges to climb over once you are in the chute.

Once you reach the rim, a 1/4 mile walk along the rim to the north-northeast will take you to a point with a fantastic view of this whole area. The Vermilion and Echo Cliffs tower over Saddle Canyon to the north. To the east are the Yon Dot Mountains and The Gap beyond them. Nankoweap drainage below Nankoweap Mesa makes up the southern view, while rising to the west is Saddle Mountain. This is a fall-winter-spring hike, with some tough scrambling at the top. As always, you will need to bring plenty of water and snack food for the journey.

22. Nankoweap Granaries and Nankoweap Mesa

There are many hikes to be done at Nankoweap, from a short easy hour-and-a-half-long hike to the Nankoweap granaries to a wonderful though difficult all-day hike to Nankoweap Mesa. For camps in this area, see the descriptions given with hike #21. You will need to start early in the day, pack a lunch and aim to be back by sunset if you are heading to Nankoweap Mesa.

To hike to the granaries, follow the well-marked path proceeding up-river from the lower three Nankoweap camps. You will come to a fork in the trail. The left fork heads up to the granaries high up at the base of the cliffs to the west. This is a wonderful moonlight hike too. To hike to Nankoweap Mesa, you need to take the right fork and follow the path north over the low hill between camp and the main Nankoweap drainage. From the Little Nankoweap Camp, you will need to walk downstream on the path leaving this camp and proceed around a low hill into the main Nankoweap drainage. Coming from either direction, once in the drainage, hike southwest upstream. You will find occasional cairned routes that make the journey a little easier. There is permanent water in the creekbed, but you should have no trouble keeping your boots dry on this section of the hike. Within 2 miles you will hike through the Butte Fault complex. As you cross the fault, the Redwall canyon falls away and you enter rolling countryside. You are going to need to leave the creek and hike southeast, but don't leave the Nankoweap drainage before you have completely passed the fault area. If you hike up the last Redwall drainage before the fault, you will be cliffed out and find the going very difficult. You will visit this drainage again today, but be patient. Stay in the creekbed until you pass the Nankoweap trail as it exits the drainage to the northwest.

After this junction, proceed another 1/4 mile or less up the creekbed and look for a small drainage coming in from the southeast. Hike up the ridge just east of this drainage, heading southeast. In about a mile you will reach the saddle between Nankoweap Mesa and Nankoweap Butte. It's another mile or so of tougher going to the mesa top. Head to the northeast, proceeding just north of a fin of broken limestone cliffs, and into the head of the drainage that you were not supposed to try to hike up in the last paragraph. Hike around the head of this drainage and pick your way up the chute in front of you to the mesa top. From here you can hike 3/4 mile north to the northeast corner of the mesa and get a great view of camp, or you can hike southeast 3/4 mile and take in the view of Malgosa Crest and Kwagunt Butte to the southeast. It's a long way back to camp from here, so don't stay long. On a hot summer day, though it's enjoyable at the mesa top, it is difficult to carry enough water and food to safely make this hike.

49

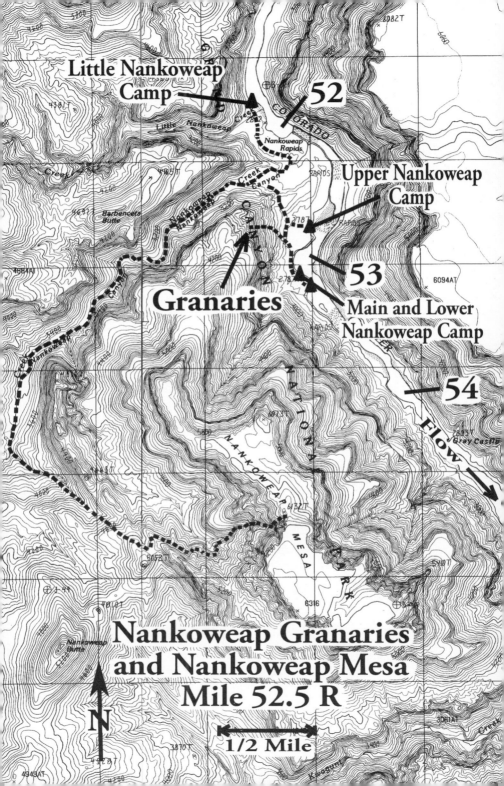

Little Nankoweap
Camp

52

Upper Nankoweap
Camp

Granaries

53

Main and Lower
Nankoweap Camp

54

Flow

**Nankoweap Granaries
and Nankoweap Mesa
Mile 52.5 R**

N

1/2 Mile

23. Nankoweap to Kwagunt Loop

There is a fine though difficult all-day loop hike that takes you all the way around Nankoweap Mesa. The best camps for this loop hike are the three lower Nankoweap camps (see hike #21). If you are camped at the Little Nankoweap camp, you could hike this loop, but the slog back to camp is a mile longer, and at the end of a long day, that mile is precious. You might want to consider seeing if the folks who stay in camp want to move the camp down to the mouth of Kwagunt Creek. Who knows why the folk on your trip might want to do this, but it's an option that would save the hikers a 3.5-mile walk back to camp at Nankoweap.

Assuming your camp is one of the lower three Nankoweap camps, and you are returning to this camp at day's end, head out of camp at first light following the well-marked path proceeding upriver. You will come to a fork in the trail. One way heads up to the granaries high up at the base of the cliffs to the west, but you need to follow the path north, and hike over the low hill between camp and the main Nankoweap drainage. Once in the drainage, hike southwest upstream. You will find occasional cairned routes that make the journey a little easier. There is permanent water in the creekbed, but you should have no trouble keeping your boots dry on this section of the hike. In a little under 2 miles you will hike through the Butte Fault complex.

As you cross the fault, the Redwall Canyon you have been hiking through falls away and you enter rolling countryside. You are going to need to leave the creek and hike southeast, but don't leave the Nankoweap drainage before you have completely passed the fault area. If you hike up the last Redwall drainage before the fault, you will be cliffed out and find the going very difficult. Be patient and stay in the creekbed until you pass the Nankoweap Trail as it exits the drainage to the northwest.

From this junction, proceed another 1/4 mile or less up the creekbed and look for a small drainage coming in from the southeast. Hike up the ridge just east of this drainage, heading southeast. In about a mile you will reach the saddle between Nankoweap Mesa and Nankoweap Butte. If it's a hot day, you may find a little shade under a few boulders, while you question the intelligence of doing this hike in the heat. There is a great view from here south into the broad Kwagunt Valley and northwest into the equally expansive Nankoweap Valley.

Dinosaur Camp

50

Flow

51

51.2 Mile Camp
51.4 Mile Camp
Little Nankoweap Camp

52

Nankoweap to Kwagunt Loop Mile 52.5 R

|← 1 Mile →|

N

Upper Nankoweap Camp

53

Main Nankoweap Camp
Lower Nankoweap Camp

54

55

56

Kwagunt Camp

23. Nankoweap to Kwagunt Loop contd.

From this saddle, you need to head 1.5 miles or more southeast down into the Kwagunt Valley, following the watercourse of a small drainage. Once in the creekbed of the main Kwagunt drainage, turn left and head 1/2 mile east into the narrows of Kwagunt Creek just east of the Butte Fault. There is usually water and shade here. From this point, it's an easy walk and a little under 2 miles back to the river.

Fortunately, you are now back at the river, with lots of cool water. Unfortunately, you are still a long way from camp. It's 3.5 miles or so back upriver, with occasional boulder hopping and route finding through thick brush. There is a small game trail the second half of the way, so look for it. The walk back to camp is much easier once you are on this game trail. This is a long all-day loop hike. River parties, both commercial and otherwise, have become lost in the country to the west of Nankoweap Mesa, with a resultant unintended night spent out in the backcountry. This is a great fall, winter or spring hike. In the middle of the summer heat, you will need lots of water and salty snack food, or enough sense not to attempt this loop.

24. Kwagunt Creek and the Kwagunt-Malgosa Loop

Kwagunt camp is a great place to stage an easy few-hour walk up Kwagunt Creek or to spend a whole day hiking a very difficult loop hike into the next drainage downriver. The camp at Mile 56.2 R at the foot of Kwagunt Rapid on river right is a great camp for early morning shade in the summer, with some midday sun in the winter.

For a short pleasant walk from this camp, head west away from the river into Kwagunt Creek. Depending on the time of year and how dry it is, you will eventually find water in the creekbed. Walk on up the drainage, which will narrow down into some limestone patios with shade in about 1.5 miles. It's a nice place to get out of the sun on a hot summer day. If you follow the creek another 1/4 mile or so, you walk across the Butte Fault and into open rolling country, as also happens in the Nankoweap drainage. The broad Kwagunt Valley opens up before you to the southwest. But wait, this is supposed to be a short pleasant walk, and you are already 2 miles from camp.

If you want to journey out for the day and get a great view while seeing a lot of country, then the Kwagunt-Malgosa loop is an option. To hike this very difficult loop, head southwest out of camp and climb right up the talus slope on creek right of the Kwagunt drainage. There is an obvious chute going through the Redwall from the top of this talus slope, and that chute is the one you go up. Keep following this chute up and along to the very top of the Redwall. It's only 1/2 mile from camp on the level. Once you have climbed through the Redwall, look for chimneys and cracks through a few cliff bands of Supai as you make your way another 1/2 mile towards the saddle between the two buttes that make up the Malgosa Crest.

Your hiking efforts to get to the crest are rewarded by a really great view. The majestic needle butte 6 miles to the west and north just a little is Mount Hayden. The view south from here to 60 Mile Rapid and the Little Colorado River Canyon is impressive as well. From here, head out west-southwest along the south side of the crest. A large portion of the crest is remarkably flat. From the southwestern corner of the crest, you now head south into the Malgosa drainage following a broken ridge of Supai. The head of the Malgosa drainage is about 1 1/2 miles from the saddle.

From here, it's a downhill walk out the Malgosa drainage. Unfortunately, you can only head down the drainage about 1/2 mile, and will need to look for a game trail heading out along the south side of the drainage (creek right) as soon as you are below the Redwall cliffs and at the top of a small waterfall. Stay at this level and traverse along this game trail past a small spring another 3/4 mile to the clear slope

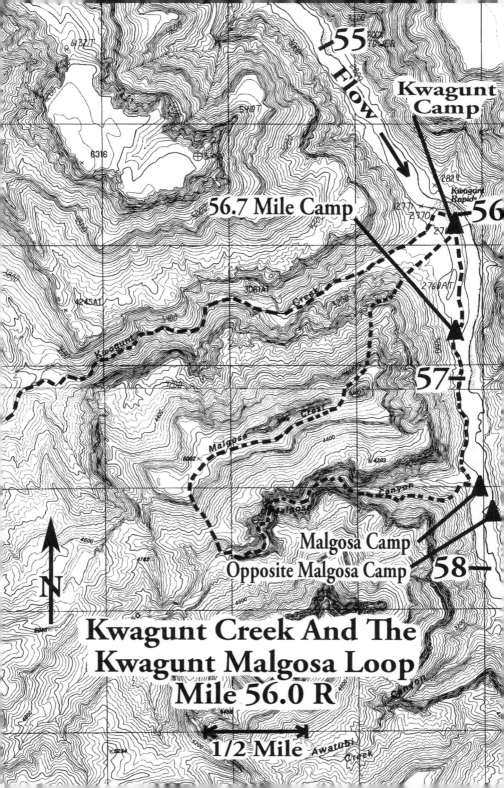

55

Flow

Kwagunt Camp

56.7 Mile Camp

56

57

Malgosa Camp
Opposite Malgosa Camp

58

N

Kwagunt Creek And The Kwagunt Malgosa Loop Mile 56.0 R

1/2 Mile

24. Kwagunt Creek and the Kwagunt Malgosa Loop contd.

leading down to the mouth of Malgosa Creek. Mind the fragile desert vegetation as you descend this slope and stay on the trail. By following this route you avoid a number of pourovers in the drainage, which leave you on steep slippery slopes with drops just below.

Once back to the river, the last hard part of this hike presents itself. Hiking the first half of the 1.5 miles back to camp is through brush and over boulders along the river. This is surprisingly difficult, especially when you add the fatigue from the journey of getting back to the river itself. Beware: do not attempt this loop in reverse, from Malgosa to Kwagunt, as it's too easy to loose the route along the way.

25. Little Colorado River and Beamer Cabin

The Little Colorado River, with blue water when not in flood, offers the Canyon traveler a few side adventures that are very enjoyable. The nearby Beamer Cabin and small riffles to play in make for a fine, short, easy hike. The mouth of the river at Mile 61.25 L offers full summer sun at lunchtime, while in winter there is cold shade here at noon. In order to protect Humpback Chub habitat, do not row your boat into the mouth of the Little Colorado River.

In the summer, it's fun to take your life jacket and head up the creek right bank of the Little Colorado 1/2 mile to some small riffles. You can float back down through these riffles with your life jacket worn around your waist like a diaper. Your jacket will protect your rear end from submerged rocks as you wash down through the riffle. Though still "cool," the waters of the Little Colorado are noticeably warmer than the water in the Colorado. On the way back to the boats you can cross to river left, and under a protective overhang look at the rock cabin built by one-time Grand Canyon prospector Ben Beamer in the 1890s. Remember, this is an archaeological ruin, and needs your help to stay in one piece. Leave what you find for others to appreciate as you do.

This stop is a very popular attraction, and you should expect others to stop in while you are here. As always, when you get the chance to chat with other river-running parties, find out where folks are planning to camp so everyone can find a room at the inn.

60

Flow

Little Colorado River Mile 61.25 L

N

3200

×4026

1/4 Mile

60.8 Mile Camp

408×

61

61 Mile Camp

×4364

Above LCR Camp

2800

Play Riffles

Pull-In

3200

LITTLE

×2953

3000-

Beamer Cabin

Below LCR low water camp

3400

62

4200

26. Temple Butte

What a fine combination: a great hike with a great camp from which to stage it. The Carbon camp at Mile 64.7 R is at the bottom of the debris fan just below the Carbon Creek riffle. This camp has good morning and evening summer shade, and fine winter sun. To hike to Temple Butte and back requires a 6-mile round-trip walk, so plan on taking the better part of a day to do this hike. All but the last 1/2 mile of this hike is easy, but that last 1/2 mile is on the very difficult end of the very difficult scale.

From camp, head up the Carbon drainage just behind camp. There are a few chockstones to climb around. This canyon gets a lot of river visitation, so look for the obvious paths and scrambles around these chockstones. In about 1/4 mile, the canyon opens up into a gravel wash, and ends in another huge pile of boulders. Creek right has a steep climb past this boulder pile, cresting a small saddle, then dropping down 50 feet to a traverse back into a narrow Tapeats Sandstone slot canyon. A few more easy scrambles up small pourovers for another 1/4 mile or more will bring you to the Butte Fault. Watch for the otherwise flat Tapeats Sandstone to suddenly bend up 90 degrees and point to the sky. There is usually a small seep here. Just a little farther and you walk right into the rolling country of the broad Chuar Valley. This is quite a contrast to the cliff-and-slope country you have been traveling through since Lees Ferry.

From here, continue up the Carbon Creek. It is very brushy in spots, but within 1/2 mile the creek turns to the north and the brush thins. In another 1/4 mile you will reach a fork. You need to continue north up the east fork of Carbon. This drainage runs between Carbon Butte to the west and Temple Butte to the east. You only want to hike up this arm of Carbon 3/4 of a mile. If you find yourself due east of Carbon Butte, you have hiked too far north.

From here, turn east and hike the 1/4 mile to the base of the Redwall cliff you have been skirting. There are at least two routes up through the limestone cliff, each route separated by a few hundred yards. If you are on route, you will be able to bench back and forth, going up chutes and ridges through the slightly broken Redwall. The northern route is marginally easier then the southern one.

Once you reach the top of the Redwall, hike another 1/4 mile southeast up toward the band of Supai Sandstone cliffs on the skyline. On the northeast corner of the bluffs made by these cliffs is a small chute that leads through the cliffs to the top. From here, a short boulder hop south takes you to the top of the butte.

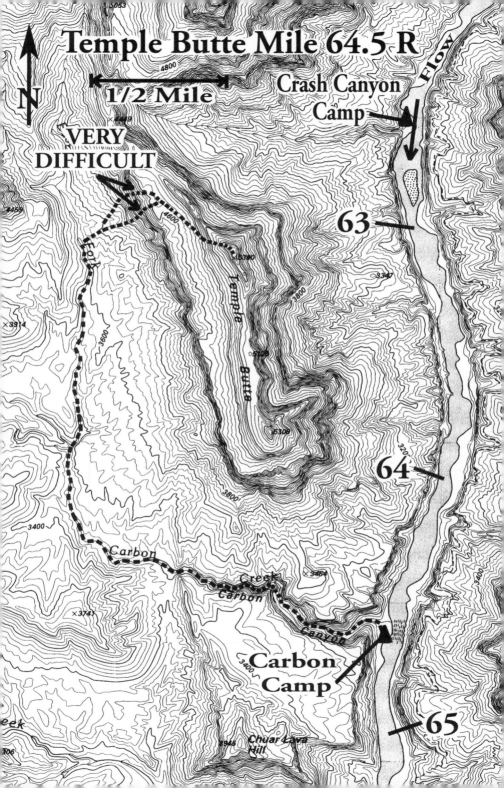

Temple Butte Mile 64.5 R

N

1/2 Mile

VERY DIFFICULT

Crash Canyon Camp

Flow

63

Temple Butte

64

Carbon Creek
Carbon

Carbon Canyon

Carbon Camp

65

Chuar Lava Hill

26. Temple Butte contd.

The high-point is on the button of Supai another 1/2 mile south, but it's only 8 feet higher and will require climbing to ascend. You will want to consider whether the extra elevation is worth an extra mile walk. There is a great view from here south into the Tanner Canyon country, west to the North Rim, north to Chuar Butte, and to the Hopi Salt Mines just to the east and across the river way down below you. This is one of those places where it is easy to spend a lot of time, as the view is so good and the climb back through the Redwall so intimidating. This is a very hot summer hike, and best attempted any time but summer. Bring plenty of water and food as usual. The hike home is the reverse of the up-climb.

27. Carbon-Chuar Loop

There are only a few popular loop hikes in Grand Canyon where you can have the hikers go off hiking on an easy route and return to the river to meet up with the boats downriver. The Carbon-Chuar loop offers just such a hike. The hikers will need to leave the boats at the Carbon camp pull-in (Mile 64.7 R), and the boat folk will need to float on another 3/4 of a mile to the pull-in at Mile 65.5 R just above Lava Canyon Rapid. There is a small eddy to pull into with a few big mesquites for shade. Some groups leave boats back up at Carbon and hike the loop in reverse, then bring the boats on down to rejoin their party. If you leave your boats, batten them down tight, as the ravens in this area are good at finding ways to get to your gear and food if left accessible. You might want to camp at the Lava Canyon pull-in. This camp has great winter sun, but is a hot one in the summer.

For those folk dropped off at the Carbon Creek mouth, the first 1/2 mile or so of the route is exactly the same as the Temple Butte hike (#26). Head on up the Carbon drainage. There are a few chockstones to climb around. This canyon gets a lot of river visitation, so look for the obvious paths and scrambles around these chockstones. In about 1/4 mile, the canyon opens up into a gravel wash, and ends in another huge pile of boulders. Creek right has a steep climb past this boulder pile, cresting a small saddle, then dropping down 50 feet to a traverse back into a narrow Tapeats Sandstone slot canyon. A few more easy scrambles up small pourovers for another 1/4 mile or more will bring you to the Butte Fault. Watch for the otherwise flat Tapeats Sandstone to suddenly bend up 90 degrees. There is usually a small seep here.

From here, you need to look for a well-used trail leaving creek right and heading south. This trail starts just past the end of the sandstone cliffs you have been hiking along, and heads up a small rise. In only a few hundred yards, the trail begins to drop into the Chuar Valley following a small drainage bottom. There is one pourover the trail goes east around. This country is a world of tilted strata and rolling hills, very different from the cliffs, slopes and tight drainages most of the routes in this book traverse. It's a little over 1/2 mile down to Lava Canyon. Chuar Valley? Lava Canyon? This drainage in Grand Canyon has two named creeks, Lava and Chuar. They join in the expansive Chuar Valley, which narrows into Lava Canyon before reaching the Colorado. Once you reach the permanent water in Lava Canyon, hike downstream 3/4 mile or so to the river and your boats. This is a popular hike, from two popular camps. Please communicate with other river trips about your intentions. A little coordination with other Canyon travelers makes everyone's adventure that much more enjoyable.

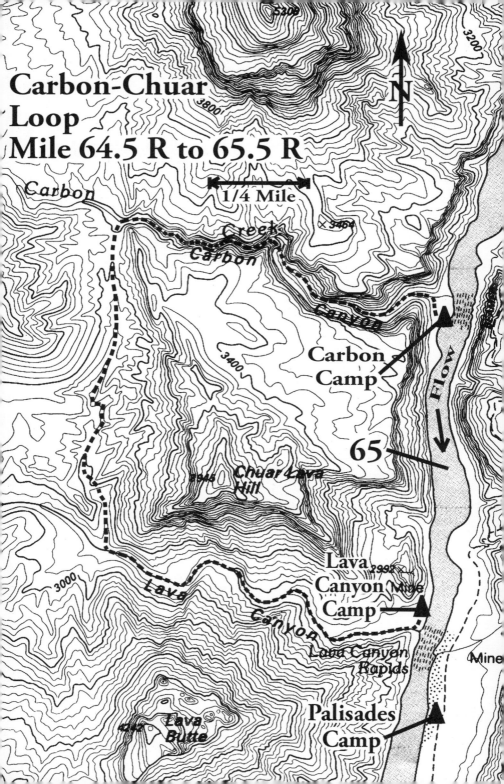

Carbon-Chuar Loop
Mile 64.5 R to 65.5 R

N

5309

3200

3800

1/4 Mile

Carbon

Creek

Carbon

× 3464

Carbon

Canyon

Carbon
Camp

3400

Flow

65

Chuar Lava
Hill

2948

Lava
Canyon
Camp

2998 ×

Mile

3000

Lava

Canyon

Lava Canyon
Rapids

Mine

Lava
Butte

4242

Palisades
Camp

28. Lava Chuar Canyon

There is a lot of country to explore west of the Colorado River up Lava Canyon and into the broad Chuar Valley. A short easy hike to the knoll above camp or longer easy hikes into the Chuar Valley offer many hiking opportunities for the river runner. The camp of choice is at Mile 65.5 R, just above Lava Canyon Rapid. The pull-in is at a small eddy with a rocky slope on the upper end and a small beach on the lower end. This camp has very good winter sun, but is a hot one in the summer.

There is a nice sunset viewpoint just out of camp. Hike up the creek-left slope behind camp for 1/10 of a mile or less, then hike north to a small saddle and back east to the top of the knoll. It's a fine view from this point.

If you have a little more time, hike up Lava Canyon and into the broad Chuar Valley. In a little over a mile you will come to a seep with large cottonwood trees. This spring was used as a water source for a moonshine factory in the 1920s, and a coffee grinder left by the distillers is now encased in a large cottonwood tree here.

From here, an enjoyable walk is to hike northwest 2 miles up the main drainage to the junction of Chuar and Lava Creeks. From this junction hike north just over 1/2 mile, then due east over a small saddle and down into the Carbon Creek drainage just over the other side of the saddle. Hike about 2.5 miles down Carbon Creek to the Butte Fault, where the broad Carbon Creek suddenly narrows and enters the tight Tapeats Sandstone narrows. Turn south on the Carbon-Chuar loop trail and hike back to the head of Lava Canyon. Retrace your steps downcanyon to camp. This is a hot valley in the summer, but an enjoyable place for a stroll on a cloudy or cool day. This is one of the few areas in Grand Canyon where you can walk a half-dozen miles or so and not have to gain or lose a lot of elevation.

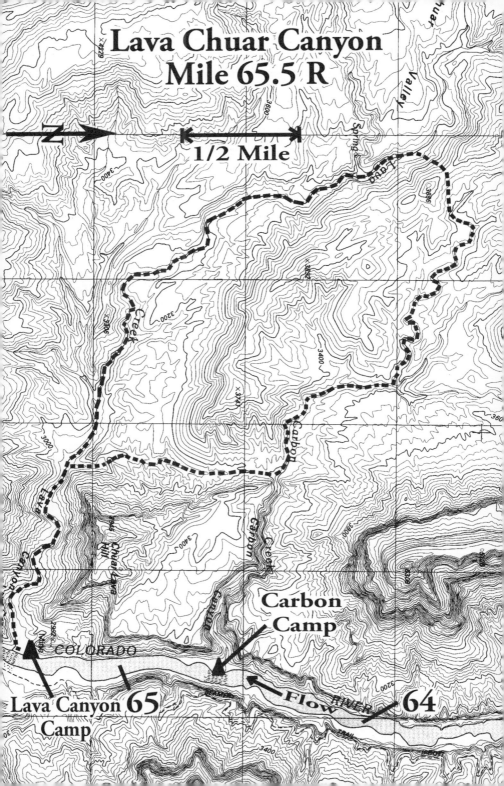

Lava Chuar Canyon
Mile 65.5 R

1/2 Mile

Spring

Valley

Creek

Carbon

Carbon Creek

Lava

Chuar Lava Hill

CANYON

Carbon

COLORADO

Carbon Camp

Flow

RIVER

Lava Canyon Camp

65

64

29. Tanner Canyon Petroglyphs & Tanner Trail to Cardenas Butte

The Tanner area offers lots of exploring opportunities, from exploring ancient Puebloan dwellings and looking at petroglyphs to climbing distant buttes. There are camps on both sides of the river at 68.4. The camp on river left often has backpackers camped there, so be ready to be very magnanimous and hospitable to these folks. You might prefer to camp just across the river at the spacious Tanner camp on river right. You can row from river right to left here, using the eddies on both sides of the river to make the crossing. Both camps are hot sunny spots in the summer, hence its nickname of "Furnace Flats."

So now that you've figured out where to camp, hiking the Tanner Trail from the river to Cardenas Butte is a fine but difficult way to spend the better part of a day. If you have camped on river left, you are ready to go. You will need to ferry across the river to the very top of the Tanner wash debris fan if you camped on river right. From here, hike just downstream to the Tanner wash and intercept the Tanner Trail. It heads up the wash 1/2 mile or so, then goes up the west side of the drainage and gradually rises toward the Redwall, which you will get to in about 2.5 miles. There is no shade around here worth the name. Up you go through the well-defined Redwall trail, and continue along the Tanner for another 3/4 mile, past the first bowl on your right and into the second. From here, turn off the trail to the north and climb up the slope of Cardenas Butte. You will need to approach the butte from the south to climb through the small band of cliffs at the very top. The view here is magical. To the west is Solomon Temple, Apollo is to the north, and the Palisades of the Desert make up the massive wall to the east. You are a ways from home so don't tarry long here. The best part of this hike is it's downhill all the way to the boats.

So you are not up for hiking to Cardenas? Well, if you camped on river right, there is a great easy walk for you. From camp, hike north to the base of the cliffs just across the huge sandbar you are on. Hike downstream just a little ways, looking for a small path. It's a mesquite jungle in here, and that path is where you want to be. The path intercepts a small drainage and goes up the drainage into a boulder pile; look for rock art here. As in any world-class museum, don't let the oils of your hands come in contact with the art. The path continues up through the rocks to the top of the bluff just north of camp. If you continue east and north around this bluff, you will come to the top of the Dox cliffs that make up the right side of the river above Furnace Flats. There is a very fine view of the Palisades and Tanner Canyon here. The way back is as you have come and covers less than a mile. It's open and hot here, so bring water and food.

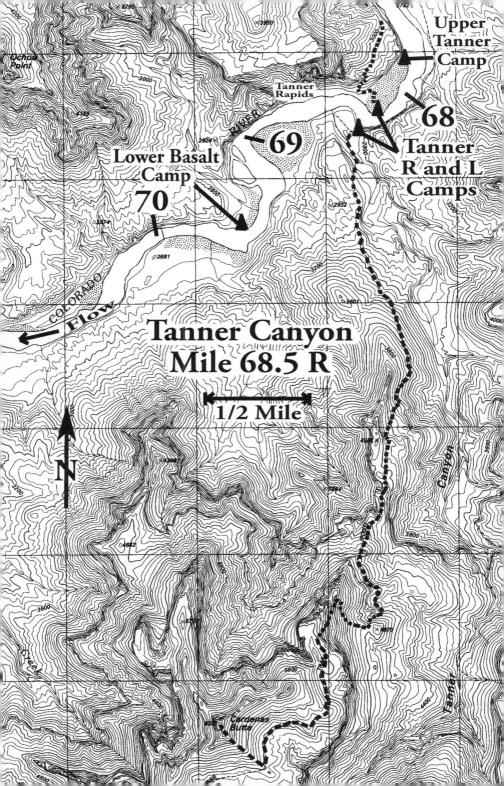

**Upper
Tanner
Camp**

Tanner
Rapids

69

68

**Tanner
R and L
Camps**

**Lower Basalt
Camp**

70

COLORADO

Flow

**Tanner Canyon
Mile 68.5 R**

1/2 Mile

N

Tanner Canyon

Cardenas
Butte

Creek

Ochoa
Point

30. Basalt Canyon, Ochoa Point, Apollo and Venus Temples

This is a really interesting area that is rarely visited. There is way too much hiking to do here in one day, from easy to very difficult, so don't bite off more then you can chew or you won't make it back to camp in time for dinner. It's really hot here in the summer, with little shade. The camp is below the Basalt Canyon riffle. There is a big eddy on river right and left. The camp is at the foot of the right eddy (Mile 69.7 R) at a small beach. There is not much protection at this camp, so if it's a stormy or windy day, camping here will be no fun. In the summer, it's going to be blistering hot. There used to be a camp upstream from the mouth of Basalt Canyon, but it is very overgrown at this writing. This is a nice winter camp, and will do fine if you want to see some wonderful country and climb to Ochoa Point and beyond to Apollo or Venus Temples.

For a short easy hike from camp, hike only a few hundred yards upstream along the river east to Basalt Canyon Creek. Once in the creek, hike northwest up the wash. In about 3/4 mile, you will come to a fork. The west fork is the bigger of the two, and goes another 1/2 mile into a huge bowl with a very impressive waterfall at the back of the bowl, the rim of which is lined with a cliff of Cardenas Basalt. This is an interesting place to look around. If you want to climb to the top of this waterfall, then the east fork is the place for you to explore. The east fork has a few salty springs in it, one of which seeps enough to keep a lone stand of cottonwood and mesquite alive in the middle of this very hot and otherwise arid drainage. If you hike up the east arm, after about 1/2 mile from the fork with the west arm, you would do well to hike out of the wash and head northwest up through a band of basalt cliffs and onto the highlands dividing the east and west drainage's of Basalt Creek. Drop down into the western arm creekbed, then walk back to the top of the waterfall on the western drainage. It is hot like the center of the earth here in the summer. The route back to camp is as you have come. Bring lots of water, salty snack food and a hat. Avoid multiple trailing and hike in the drainage bottoms as much as possible. Try to stay off the large dunes here as well, as your footprints will stay in them for a long time.

To attempt the very difficult 3 1/2 mile hike to the temples Venus and Apollo by way of Ochoa Point, you'll need to hike to Ochoa Point first. Ochoa is only 1 1/2 miles away and a couple of thousand feet straight up. To get there, hike northwest out of camp, climbing up to the top of the gravel bluff that faces camp. From here, continue northwest for 1 mile or so following the ridge top directly towards Ochoa Point. You will be heading toward a chute going up into the Cardenas Basalt's. Proceed up this chute to its top at a small saddle, then to

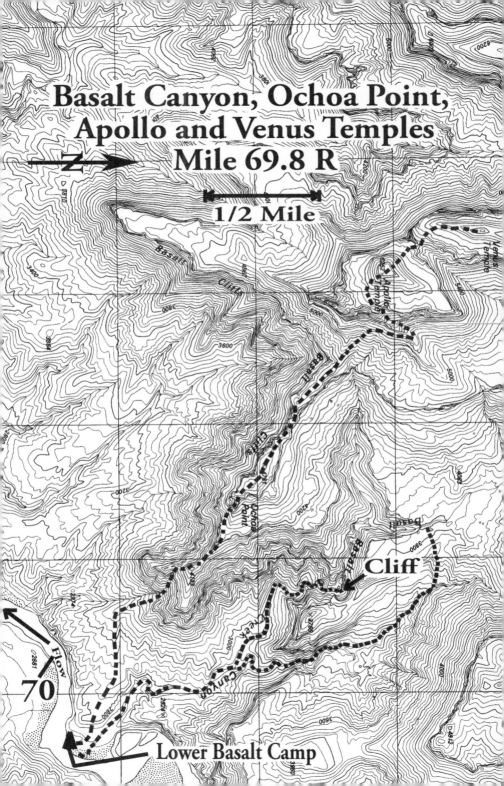

Basalt Canyon, Ochoa Point, Apollo and Venus Temples Mile 69.8 R

1/2 Mile

Basalt Cliffs

Basalt

Basalt Cliffs

Ochoa Point

Apollo Temple

Venus Temple

Basalt

Cliff

Creek Canyon

Flow

70

Lower Basalt Camp

the north, working your way to the northeast side of the Ochoa ridge, then cut back to the south side of this ridge. There's a break through the Tapeats Sandstone here that will take you up to the top of the Tapeats with only a little very difficult ledge work close to the top of the climb through the Tapeats.

From Ochoa Point (yes, it is an impressive view from here) head northwest along the top of what's called the Basalt Cliffs for another mile toward Apollo Temple. There's one small divide you will have to drop down into and climb back out of in less then 1/2 mile from Ochoa Point. Once you begin to climb up onto the side of Apollo, head to the north 1/8 mile, then follow a small drainage back up to the west right up through the Redwall. You will top out of the Redwall only 1/4 mile from the summit of Apollo, now to the northwest. It's an easy walk over to Apollo's crest from here. The top of Apollo has some very interesting erosional features at the very top, in that the Supai Sandstone has eroded into multiple small hills and valleys of sandstone. So how about this view? Cardenas Creek is just to the south, with the Tabernacle to the southwest. Vishnu Temple is just to your west, with the Palisades of the Desert to the east, and Temple and Chuar Buttes to the northeast. This is a stunning spot.

If you are doing okay for time, food, water, stamina and weather, you might want to wander over to Venus Temple, less than a mile to the north. Hike down to the Venus-Apollo saddle, then on back up to the summit of Venus. Please note that if you decide to hike from Venus north over to Jupiter on top of the Redwall, you will have to cross a razor's edge ridge of Redwall. There will be a number of climbing moves required here, and this more-than-very-difficult route has a lot of exposure. The summit of Venus is a great place to hang out for a while, count your blessings, then head on back to camp. You are a long way from home up here.

31. Hilltop Ruins and Unkar Overlook

The Hilltop Ruins and Unkar Rapid Overlook offer an easy afternoon walk, especially if there is a little cloud cover. The camp at the Cardenas marsh, though often overgrown with camel thorn, has fine views of the Palisades of the Desert at sunset. This is one of those "Heart of the Canyon" spots. The pull-in at Mile 71.1 L is quick and small, just around a small bar edging into the river. The Cardenas camp is just upstream of a large grove of Gooding willow, though the beaver here continue to chew them down faster than these big trees can grow. This camp has a number of secluded campsites surrounded by arrowweed and protected from the wind.

There is a path leading south out of camp, through some mesquite covered sand dunes, and up onto a bench roughly 200 yards out of camp. This trail intersects the Escalante Trail. From here, you can enjoy a walk on high bluffs east back toward Tanner on the Escalante Trail, continue south and explore the Cardenas Creek drainage, or take the Escalante Trail to your right (west) and climb up and around to the Hilltop Ruin Trail.

To climb to the Hilltop Ruin, from the junction of the Cardenas camp trail with the Escalante Trail, turn west (downriver) and climb up the low hill in front of you. After only a few hundred feet, look for a small trail going up the hill and leave the main Escalante Trail at this point. Continue up the hill to its top, where you will see the remains of a structure that has endured since Ancestral Puebloan time. As with all archaeological ruins, don't mess with the walls. They have lasted through time because countless Canyon visitors have left them alone. The views from here are magnificent. To the north is Apollo Temple, with the long lines of cliffs to the east called the "Palisades of the Desert," and Vishnu Temple dominating the western skyline.

Proceed southwest along the ridge leading away from the hilltop and into a small bowl where you cross the Escalante Trail, and hike back west to the cliffs above Unkar Rapid. You are rewarded with a fine view of the Unkar Creek delta ruins complex and Unkar Rapid a few hundred feet below you. Remember to exercise caution at the cliff's edge, especially in windy conditions. The return journey can be accomplished by retracing your walk back to the Escalante route. Follow it north as it winds back down around the Hilltop Ruin knoll and then east, back to the Cardenas Camp Trail. You can easily spend an enjoyable afternoon here and cover a whole 2 miles. On a cloudless hot day there will be no shade.

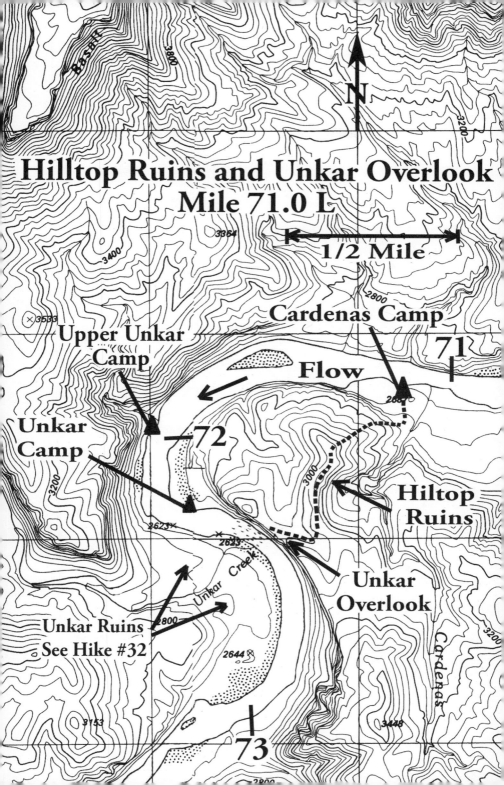

Hilltop Ruins and Unkar Overlook
Mile 71.0 L

1/2 Mile

Cardenas Camp

Upper Unkar
Camp

Flow

71

72

Unkar
Camp

Hiltop
Ruins

Unkar
Overlook

Unkar Ruins
See Hike #32

73

32. Unkar Creek

A lot of hiking can be done from the Unkar Delta. There are short and long easy hikes to some of the most extensive ancestral Puebloan dwellings in Grand Canyon, or long hikes way north into remote regions of the Unkar drainage. Whatever your hiking fancy, you'll find it here. The camp at Mile 71.9 R just above Unkar is a great camp for staging a long hike up Unkar Creek, with early afternoon shade and a great view of sunset light on the Palisades of the Desert to the east. This camp was hit hard by a flash flood some years back and is not what it used to be. You can also stop for a brief visit by pulling in a couple of hundred yards·above Unkar Rapid at Mile 72.25+ R, where a small rocky beach opens just below a thicket of tall Phragmites reeds.

To see the ancient Puebloan dwellings, either walk downstream from camp 1/4 mile to the Unkar Delta or hike up the trail from the beach. Once on top of the delta, there is an extensive network of trails going to dwellings on both sides of the Unkar drainage. The largest dwelling complex is on the south side of the drainage, and is reached by the trail going away from the Colorado up a small rise, where it turns south to cross the large Unkar drainage, only 1/4 mile from the boat beach.

The Unkar drainage, with permanent water only within the first few miles, is a large, easily hiked drainage. You can hike the 1/2 mile up to the water and look for shade, or go much farther on into the wide Unkar valley. There will be no shade up here in the summer. This wonderful half-day hike is great in the fall, winter or spring. Be sure to bring enough water and food for the day.

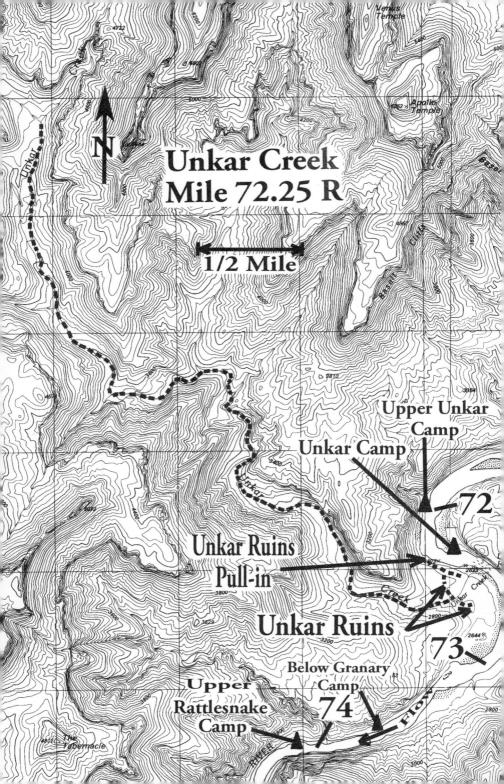

Unkar Creek
Mile 72.25 R

N

1/2 Mile

Venus
Temple

Apollo
Temple

Basalt
Cliffs

Unkar
Creek

Upper Unkar
Camp

Unkar Camp

**Unkar Ruins
Pull-in**

72

Unkar Ruins

73   2644

Below Granary
Camp

74

**Upper
Rattlesnake
Camp**

The
Tabernacle

RIVER   FLOW

33. The Tabernacle Route

The Palisades of the Desert is an extensive line of cliffs that run from the confluence of the Little Colorado River south to the old Tanner Trail in Tanner Canyon. With massive walls that make up the tail end of the East Rim before the rim turns west, the Palisades are impressive from camps like Basalt (Mile 69.7 R) or Cardenas (Mile 71.0 L). Trouble is, it's hard to get a view of the Palisades of the Desert from the Inner Gorge. There is a great easy hike, just before the Inner Gorge, that offers a stunning view of the Palisades. It's a real Sistine Chapel view, and appropriately, this is the hike to the Tabernacle.

The camps where you will need to stay to do this hike are between River Mile 73.6 and 74.3, all on river right. There are three camps here. The pull-ins are easy and the camps spacious. This route starts at the Upper Rattlesnake camp at Mile 74.1 R. You can access this point from Lower Rattlesnake at Mile 74.3 R by walking back upriver. If you are camped at Below Granary camp at Mile 73.6 R, walk downriver a bit.

Look for cairns that mark the start of the route as it goes up to a sharp ridge of Dox Sandstone just downstream (west) from the mouth of the drainage that enters river right at 74.0. The route continues up this exposed ridge line, which turns to the west. The ridge top widens out as the trail turns southwest and enters the Tapeats Sandstone. Pay close attention to the route here and try to avoid multiple trailing to protect the fragile Canyon soils. Once the trail tops out of the Tapeats and enters the Bright Angel Shale, the route proceeds west around the north side of the Tabernacle to a small saddle. The route then turns southwest as it winds around and up the west side of the Tabernacle and on to the top. At the top, you will be in the Muav Limestone.

From here, to the south is Solomon Temple between you and Hance Rapid. To the west is Sheba Temple, while north of you and just a bit west is Rama Shrine. North and a little east are the distant Apollo, Venus and Jupiter Temples, all cradled in the outstretched arms of the Palisades, forming your skyline to the east. What a view!

This is a great early morning, late afternoon or full moon hike, taking three to four hours. Keep in mind there is no shade except in the Tapeats section, and you'd be nuts to do this hike in the middle of a hot summer day. As always, stay hydrated and eat salty snack food.

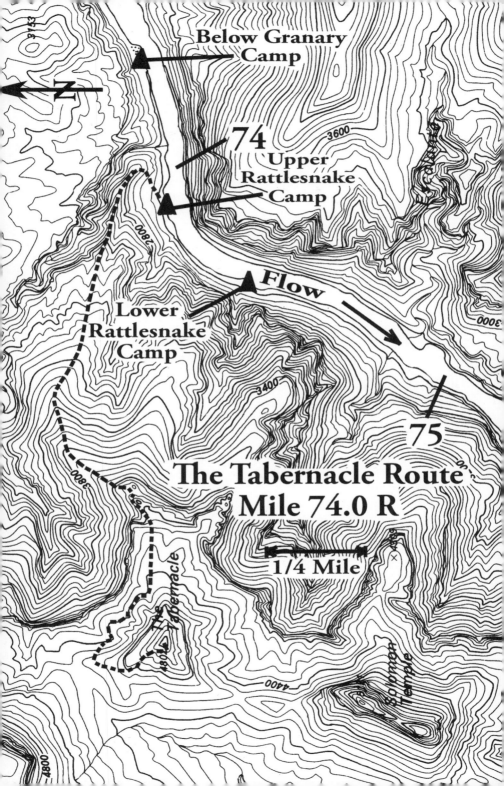

Below Granary
Camp

N

74
Upper
Rattlesnake
Camp

2800

Flow

Lower
Rattlesnake
Camp

3400

75

The Tabernacle Route
Mile 74.0 R

1/4 Mile

3800

The Tabernacle

4800

Solomon
Temple

4400

4800

3000

3600

34. 75 Mile Creek

There is a wonderful easy hike at 75 Mile Creek, just above Nevills Rapid, at Mile 75.5 L. This canyon is hiked as a short easy walk during a lunch stop, or can be hiked as a more difficult half-day hike from a nice camp at the foot of Nevills Rapid, at Mile 75.6 L. You can pull in a short 50 yards or so above the rapid and enjoy the shade of some Gooding willows for lunch.

From the upper pull-in, follow the trail behind the large willow trees to the mouth of 75 Mile Creek. The drainage goes southeast for 1/8 of a mile or less, then turns hard right to the southwest for another 1/8 of a mile or so, then back to the southeast. It's an impressive tight narrows in the Grand Canyon Supergroup rock unit called the Shinumo Quartzite. The easy hike stops here.

Folks who want a little more of a challenge will need to scramble up the creek left side of a 12-foot pourover. There is a route around this pour over on creek right if you walk back downstream a few hundred feet. This route goes up a chute to the top of the Quartzite, about 100 feet above the creek bed. There is a cairned path in this chute. At the top of the chute, a small path benches back into the creek. If you stay in the creek bed and climb past the 12-foot pourover, continue up the creek bed. You will encounter a couple more small pourovers. In another 1/4 mile, 75 Mile opens up into a broad valley.

In the fall, winter and spring of wet years, you will find water in the deeper narrows here. The Escalante Trail crosses 75 Mile Canyon here as well, so be ready to spot a backpacker or two. You can be most hospitable to backpackers by offering to take any unwanted trash they might have. You are only two miles and 4400 feet below Papago Point here. The view up to the rim is humbling. The route back to the boats is as you have come.

Below Granary Camp

Upper Rattlesnake Camp

Lower Rattlesnake Camp

74

75 Mile Creek
Mile 75.5 L

Flow

1/4 Mile

Nevills Camp

75

76

Papago Camp

N

35. Vishnu Creek

Vishnu Creek is a wonderful side canyon, rarely visited by river parties. The reasons it's so rarely visited are three. The first is that it's easy to miss the pull-in. The second is that river camps in this area are few. If you pull in to visit Vishnu Creek, you decrease your chances of getting across the river to Grapevine Camp, directly across the river from the mouth of Vishnu Creek. Lastly, with Grapevine Rapid just below Vishnu Creek, once you leave Vishnu and head on downriver, there's a big rapid to run.

Regardless of these considerations, Vishnu Creek has permanent water flowing through a tight meandering canyon whose lower canyon walls consist of Vishnu Schist. You'll need to work hard to not miss the pull-in, and really hard to keep your feet dry if you explore Vishnu Creek. You'll also want to explore this creek with at least a couple of good rock scramblers to help others not so skilled with the occasional 8-foot-high waterfalls you will encounter.

To make the pull-in at Vishnu Creek, look for a small waterfall entering the river at Mile 80.5 L. In another 1/2 mile downriver from the Cottonwood Waterfall, you will approach a small riffle. This is your only clue to pull in on river right, just above this riffle at 81.2 R. There is a small patch of sand, and a sloping wall of Vishnu Schist. Tie up, get a little water and snack food, some footwear you can get wet, and climb up away from the boats, heading downstream to the small saddle 70 feet above the river. There is a small trail here, so please stay on it. At the saddle, you will see Vishnu Creek just below you, but you will have to climb down the 70 feet into the creek bottom. Look for a small chute heading down to the creek bed. Mind that you don't step on any native vegetation here.

Once you are in Vishnu Creek, the exploration begins. In a few hundred yards you will come to the first of a series of pools and waterfalls you will need to team climb. In another mile or so you will need to bypass a 50 foot high waterfall. Use the path on creek right to hike up and round this waterfall. In a little over 1 1/2 miles, the creek bottom widens out as you enter the Tapeats Sandstone. Further exploration of a lot of very fine country is possible from this point. Keep in mind, you will not want to explore this canyon in monsoon season, and if you are still some large rapids away from camp, don't tarry too long here.

Vishnu Creek
Mile 81.2 R

1/2 Mile

N

Hall
Butte

Newberry
Butte

Granite Flow

Gorge

81

Grapevine Camp

80

36. Clear Creek

In the heat of summer, when the schist is too hot to touch, an easy hike to the wet, cool, shady Clear Creek narrows and falls can add a lot to your travels through the Upper Granite Gorge. The pull-in for this hike is easy to miss. Just below 83 Mile Rapid, the river bends slightly to the west northwest. There is a small eddy on river right at this bend (Mile 83.9 R) with a tiny sand pile on river right. The pull-in is here. A nice, but hard to find, trail with a lot of rock work (thanks to the NPS trail crew) goes downstream from here a few hundred yards, then over a schist ridge and into Clear Creek. If you blow the pull-in, don't panic. Just below the next riffle, but well above Zoroaster Rapid, there is a small boulder bar at Mile 84.25 R. From here there is a trail as well, going up into the schist and along upriver to round the corner, traversing back into Clear Creek. You could camp at either of these pull-ins, but they are very small low water camps at the best of times.

Once in the drainage, you will find a permanent clear stream of cool water with a path leading up the canyon. You will cross and re-cross the stream a number of times as you walk the 1/2 mile or so up through twisting narrows to a wonderful waterfall with a great side-flowing jet of water. This is also a highly visited site, so be ready to share this magical place with other visitors.

You can climb above the falls on creek right, but use caution as the climb is exposed and slippery. It's another 3 miles of boulder hopping and creek crossing through twisting narrows to the Clear Creek Trail coming overland 6 miles from Phantom Ranch. You don't want to explore this narrow drainage in monsoon season.

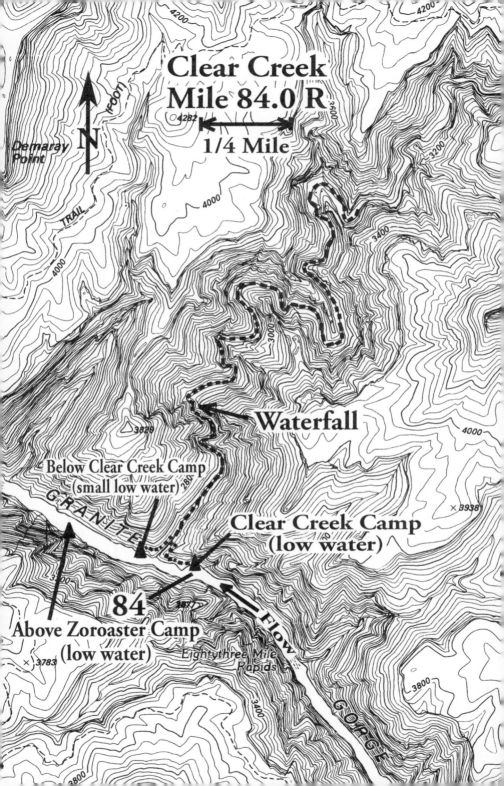

Clear Creek
Mile 84.0 R

← 1/4 Mile →

Demaray Point

N

TRAIL
(FOOT)

Waterfall

Below Clear Creek Camp
(small low water)

GRANITE

Clear Creek Camp
(low water)

84

Above Zoroaster Camp
(low water)

Flow

Eightythree Mile Rapids

GORGE

37. Phantom Ranch and Pipe Creek

There actually is some very nice easy hiking to be done in the Phantom area. Try a short hike to the canteen at the lodge for lemonade and a mail drop or head up to the Clear Creek Trail overlook.

Most folks who are exchanging passengers at Phantom Ranch try to camp at either upper or lower Cremation Camps (Mile 87.1 L, 87.2L). These two camps are separated by a small riffle, and both share the same small side canyon debris fan. These camps are the choice for passenger exchanges, as they are a five-minute float from the Kaibab suspension bridge and boat beach just below that at Mile 87.5 R. Camps between Hance Rapid 10 miles upriver and Phantom Ranch are few. If you are not exchanging passengers, you'd be helping out a lot by not camping below Hance at any of the three good and two marginal camps in this reach.

If you are camping at Cremation and are exchanging folks, you can let those who want to sleep late stay in camp and enjoy the morning shade while you take the hikers on down to the boat beach or Pipe Creek. If your hikers are going up the South Kaibab Trail, you'll want to pull in at the boat beach just past the black Kaibab suspension bridge. Folks who are taking the Kaibab Trail to the South Rim can hike up the 50 yards of short trail along the draw from the beach to the main Kaibab Trail. From here, they hike over to the black Kaibab suspension bridge and are on their way along the 7 miles of trail to the rim. It can be fun to hike up the South Kaibab with those hiking out and then turn around when you meet the folks hiking in.

If your party is hiking up the Bright Angel Trail, then you can save them a 1.5 mile walk by floating on down to the mouth of Pipe Creek. The pull-in (Mile 88.75+ L) is a little tricky, and is on river left. You will need to be in mid-current to avoid the eddy on river left at the last bend in the river just 100 yards above Pipe Creek, then move quickly to the river left shore where a small gravel beach is just above the mouth of the creek. There is a floor-ripping sleeper in this eddy, and a strainer at the lower end as well. From this beach, hike downstream just around the corner into the mouth of the Pipe Creek drainage and intercept the Bright Angel Trail. It's 7 miles up to the South Rim from here. You could hike up the trail with those leaving and return with those who are hiking in.

If you want to hike to Phantom Ranch from the boat beach, hike west less than 1/4 mile along the Boat Beach Trail, past the boaters' bulletin board and water tap to the Kaibab Trail. You can fill up your 6 gallon water jugs with drinking water here, by the way. Continue on west

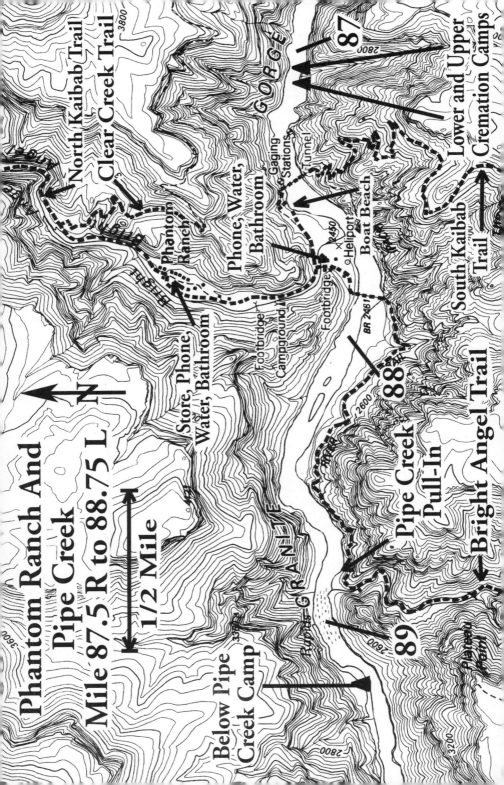

Phantom Ranch And
Pipe Creek
Mile 87.5 R to 88.75 L

1/2 Mile

N

North Kaibab Trail

Clear Creek Trail

Phantom Ranch

Phone, Water, Bathroom

Store, Phone, Water, Bathroom

Footbridge

Footbridge

Campground

Gaging Stations

Tunnel

Boat Beach

Heliport

450

GORGE

87

2800

3800

2800

Lower and Upper
Cremation Camps

South Kaibab Trail

Bright Angel Trail

Pipe Creek
Pull-In

88

BR 2461'

2600

GRANITE

Rapids

Below Pipe
Creek Camp

89

2600

2800

3200

3600

3376'

Plateau
Point

37. Phantom Ranch and Pipe Creek contd.

another few hundred yards to the junction of the Kaibab and Bright Angel Trails. There is a small footbridge over Bright Angel Creek here. Just over this bridge, on the east side of the trail, are a water spigot, bathrooms and a pay telephone. If you are at Pipe Creek and want to hike back to Phantom Ranch, hike into the mouth of Pipe Creek to the Bright Angel Trail, turn left and hike east 1.5 miles to the junction with the Kaibab Trail. You will pass the pay phone, water spigot and bathrooms on your right just before you cross the Bright Angel Creek footbridge and intercept the Kaibab Trail.

From the trail junction, head up the trail into Bright Angel Canyon. In 1/2 mile or so, you will pass the Phantom Ranch ranger station on your right, then come to a junction with a sign pointing to the right saying Phantom Ranch. You can go this way, but it passes right by the mule stop, and is not a pretty path to walk. If you go left at the sign and hike another 100 yards, you will pass behind a few of the Phantom Ranch cabins. Look for a small path heading off to your right leading to a stone building with steps at its front. This is the Phantom Ranch canteen.

There is a water spigot here too, and another around the east side of the building with bathrooms and a pay phone. In the canteen, besides Phantom Ranch T-shirts, postcards and lemonade, there is a box holding river mail. If you want to receive mail here, the river address is your name c/o Phantom Ranch River Mail, PO Box 1266, Phantom Ranch, AZ 86023. It takes an extra 3 to 4 days for mail to arrive here. As the post comes in by mule, you may be charged an extra fee for parcels. There is also a mailbag for outgoing mail. Look around by the mailbag for the rubber stamp saying "Mailed by Mule from the Bottom of the Grand Canyon" and stamp this on your outbound letters.

But enough of this foolishness with phones and flush toilets. Hike out the back of the ranch heading north. You will intercept the North Kaibab Trail. It's 14 miles to the North Rim from here. This may be why almost all exchange folks hike in or out the South Rim trails. In another 1/2 mile you will come to the Clear Creek Trail on your right. Take the Clear Creek Trail another 1/2 mile up almost to the base of the Tapeats, where the trail turns into the main Colorado River corridor. There are some great solid stone benches in the Schist here, with a fine view of the Ranch below and the South Rim across the river. It's too hot a place to walk to in the summer, but this is a great way to spend a winter exchange day at Phantom. As always, you will need water and some food for these walks.

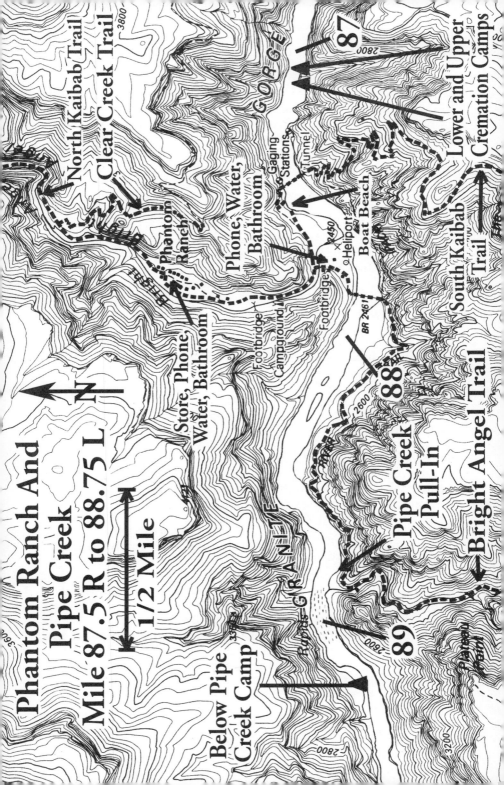

Phantom Ranch And Pipe Creek
Mile 87.5 R to 88.75 L

N

1/2 Mile

North Kaibab Trail

Clear Creek Trail

Phantom Ranch

Store, Phone, Water, Bathroom

Phone, Water, Bathroom

Gaging Stations

Tunnel

Boat Beach

Heliport

Footbridge

Footbridge

Campground

BR 450

BR 461

GORGE

GRANITE

Bright Angel

2600

2600

2800

3200

3600

3800

3400

Rapids

Below Pipe Creek Camp

Pipe Creek Pull-In

89

88

87

2800

Lower and Upper Cremation Camps

South Kaibab Trail

Bright Angel Trail

Plateau Point

38. 91 Mile Creek and the Shiva-Isis Saddle

There is a great little camp at Mile 91.1 R with winter sun and a wonderful difficult hike up 91 Mile Creek all the way to the Shiva-Isis Saddle. The camp here is the first good camp on river right below Horn Creek. You can't see the camp as you approach, as a projection of Vishnu Schist obscures the beach till you are right next to it. You can't get to Trinity Creek from here by hiking along the 1/4 mile of river that separates these two drainages, but you can hike through the schist and up onto the Tonto. You can also hike from here to the Shiva-Isis Saddle.

From camp, you will want to hike up the drainage that enters the river right next to the beach where you are camped. In 100 yards you will encounter the first of a series of small pourovers that you will have to hike around. Look for cairns marking the route around the pourovers. In 1/2 mile from the river, you will come to a major pourover. The route around this pourover is on creek right. As with every hike, follow the trail and avoid multiple trailing. In 3/4 mile you will hike out of the schist and into the Grand Canyon Supergroup Hakatai Shale Formation. The canyon bottom opens up. This is a nice open area and in the fall, winter or spring, you might want to just hang out here.

If the Shiva-Isis Saddle is your goal, in a little over 1 mile from the river, a tributary will enter the drainage from the northwest. Head up the gravel bottom 1 mile to a low saddle, then northwest to the next unnamed drainage and bay. Hike around this bay, continuing northwest, then north again another mile into the next drainage. This drainage has its head at the Shiva-Isis saddle. It's another 3/4 mile up this drainage to the saddle. You will need to do a little scrambling to get through the very top of the Redwall. The easiest way through the Redwall is at the very end of this drainage.

What a fantastic view awaits you. The Tower of Set, Horus and Osiris Temple are to the west, the deep Phantom Creek is to the east, Tiyo Point is to your north, and the Colonade is just across the way to the northeast. Views around these parts just don't get much better than this. You are a long way from the boats, and in the summer you only want to be here in your dreams. Save this hike for a cool fall, winter or spring day. Remember to avoid walking on desert crust soils, bring plenty of water and snacks, and plan on this hike taking 4 to 6 hours at least.

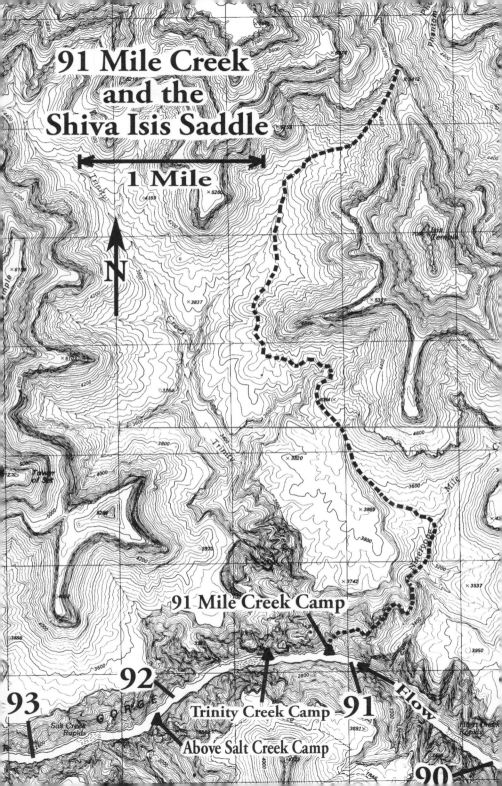

91 Mile Creek
and the
Shiva Isis Saddle

1 Mile

N

91 Mile Creek Camp

92

93

Trinity Creek Camp — 91

Above Salt Creek Camp

Flow

90

39. Trinity Creek

The cool narrows of Trinity Creek offer at least a little respite from the intense heat of the Inner Gorge in the summer. An easy walk from a small camp offers a fine short side hike here.

There is a small camp at the lower end of the equally small debris fan at the mouth of Trinity Creek (Mile 91.6 R). You will need to be ready to pull in here, as it's easy to float on by. It will be too late to get to the eddy at the foot of the riffle if you are not right on it. There is also a camp at the mouth of 91 Mile Creek. The camp at 91 Mile is a little bigger, but you can't walk along the river from there to Trinity Creek just under 1/4 mile downstream (see hike #38).

For those who want to take a short easy walk, it's only a little over 1/2 mile to the unclimbable waterfall in the tight, shade-soaked narrows that await you. In the spring there may be a trickle of water here as well. This is a great spot to escape the summer heat for a little while. You will not want to hike here in monsoon season. The same holds true for camping here.

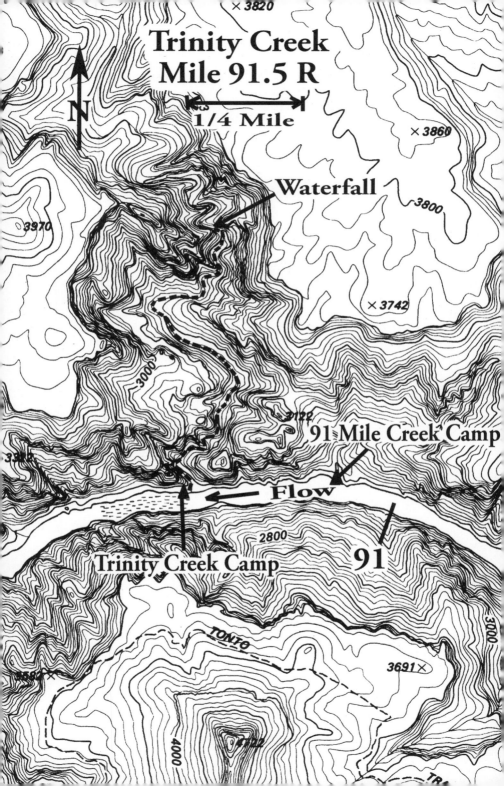

40. Monument Creek

Water, shade, a great camp, short and long hikes—what more could you ask for? The camp (Mile 93.4 L) on river left at the very top of Granite Rapid offers all this. This camp has early morning shade, and winter sun if you walk out onto the Monument Creek debris fan. This camp receives a lot of use by both boaters and backpackers. As with any beach, leave it cleaner than when you came. If you find trash left by others, please pack it out in your boat. If you have the space, you could offer the use of your groover to backpackers who are camping near you. If you really want to make the day of backpackers, offer to haul out their trash!

Hikes from camp are many. There is an easy few-hour to half-day loop hike with summer shade and a small stream. To hike from this camp, walk downriver the stone's throw to the Monument drainage, and head up the drainage. You will quickly find a bubbling stream in the canyon bottom. In about 3/4 mile, there is a small drainage with a trail in it entering from creek left. You will come down this trail as you complete the loop. Stay in the creekbed, and in another 100 yards or so you will enter some wonderful narrows. It's a great spot to hang in the shade and enjoy the water.

From here you can proceed another 1/4 mile or less through the narrows. Bring some sandals as it is wet in here. As soon as the narrows end, there is a trail leading away from the creek on creek left, up to a composting toilet for Monument Camp use. Put your boots back on, join the Monument Trail and hike back west 1/4 mile or so down into the small drainage you passed on your way up. This trail will take you past the stone tower called the Monument that gives this area its name. Once you rejoin Monument Creek, it's 3/4 mile back to the river and camp.

Those who want a longer, difficult hike can continue on up the Monument drainage another 1/4 mile to the Monument Trail. It's 8 miles east to Indian Gardens and 2 miles west to the Hermit Trail. If you walk west on the Monument Trail 1 1/2 miles, then north 1/4 mile to the edge of the Tapeats, there is a fine view of the Inner Gorge, with a great view of the Tower of Ra, Osiris Temple and the Tower of Set just a few miles away to the north. Be sure to avoid stepping on the fragile desert plants at this magnificent overlook. The route home is as you have come. In the summer, the heat here is oven-hot. Be sure to bring plenty of water and snack foods.

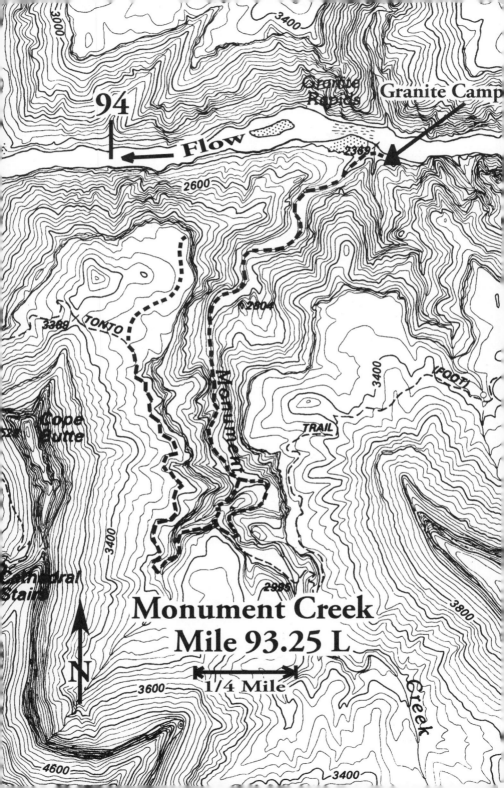

94

Granite Rapids

Granite Camp

← **Flow**

2600

2369

○ 2904

TONTO

3369

Monument

Cope Butte

3400

(FOOT)

TRAIL

2986

3400

Cathedral Stairs

3400

3800

Monument Creek
Mile 93.25 L

N

3600

1/4 Mile

Creek

4600

3400

41. 94 Mile Creek and the Hermit Fault Route

The camp at 94 Mile is not one of the "ten best" in Grand Canyon. It is prone to serious flooding in monsoon season, and then there's the all-important pull-in at Mile 94.3 R. Once you have cleared the tail waves of Granite (yikes!), there is a 1/2 mile float on down to the next riffle. This is the 94 Mile drainage. Pull in above the riffle on the right and scout this camp out. There's a kitchen spot sometimes on the lower end of the debris fan, but you may have to line the boats down one at a time to get there. Once you've done all that work, most of the rest of this camp is in the gravel stream bed, so don't camp here in monsoon season.

Still, access to a fantastic variety of winter hikes is what this camp is all about. The two peaks you can see due north in the sunset are Osiris Temple and the Tower of Ra. There they are, so close, just up 94 Mile. Up to the time of this printing, no one has yet documented a ropeless route out the north end of 94 Mile through the Redwall. Still, 94 Mile has some fine schist narrows 1 1/2 miles up the drainage. There's one small pourover about 1/2 mile from the river, which is easily bypassed on creek right. In a little over another 1/2 mile, the gravel streambed is replaced by Vishnu Schist, with some impressive small intrusions of Zoroaster Granite. There's a sloping waterfall next, and then a small section of schist narrows. This is followed by an unclimable pourover at about 1 1/2 miles from the river. You can bypass this waterfall on the right or left sides, though creek right is easier. There's a small spring just above this point. The drainage turns gravel here for another 1/2 mile till you reach the top of the Tapeats, where there are some easily passable small pourovers. There's a fork in the drainage here. If you proceed north up the northern arm less than 1/2 mile, you will be cliffed out by very impressive Redwall. For a more difficult hike to the south fin of the Tower of Set, proceed east out of camp (upriver) 1/4 mile to intersect the Hermit Fault. Proceed northeast another 1/4 mile right up the fault through the Tapeats Sandstone to the Tonto. From here, continue to proceed northeast, being careful to avoid stepping on the abundant Mojave prickly-pear cactus. In another 1/2 mile you will cross a small divide, and the Hermit Fault break in the Redwall will be visible another mile to the northeast. Stay in the drainage as you hike up through this Redwall break, and mind the catclaw acacia. Once you top out of the Redwall, proceed south 1/2 mile along the south fin of the Tower of Set. You will pass a small natural arch on the east side of this fin. At the fin's tip is a view of the inner canyon that makes up for the camp at 94 Mile. Set is to your north, Isis to your northeast, and the Inner Gorge to your east, south and west. The return is as you have come. This is not a summer hike. Period. You will need enough food and water for the day.

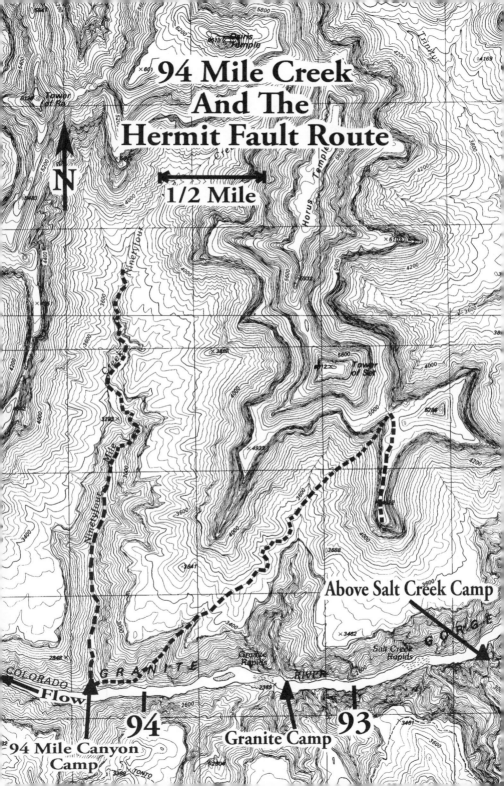

94 Mile Creek
And The
Hermit Fault Route

N

1/2 Mile

Above Salt Creek Camp

COLORADO
Flow

94

93

94 Mile Canyon Camp

Granite Camp

42. Crystal Creek to Osiris Temple

There is a lot more to do at the Crystal Rapid camp (Mile 98.0 R) than worry about running the rapid. Why sweat it when you can go for a wonderful hike, from easy to very difficult. The camp at Crystal is actually fairly nice, with campsites spread along the high water line from 50 yards into the Schist at the upper end of the debris fan down to the scout pull-in. The hiking from here on up the Crystal drainage, is very enjoyable. There is permanent water in the creekbed. Remember that most river trips will stop here for the scout of Crystal, so if you are considering a layover here, be ready to share your camp with other river runners.

You can hike for a few hours here or all day. From camp, hike up to the top of the debris fan behind camp, and walk into the mouth of Crystal Creek. There is a small path leading down into the creekbed. From here it is an easy, mile-long walk up to a landslide that has recently choked the creek and made a nice little waterfall. This is a good place to "hang out" and then head back, unless you have food and water for the day. The drainage is open and hot in the summer, without a lot of shade.

If you are willing to attempt a very difficult adventure, then plan a layover. For this hike you will want to pack a flashlight, as you may be returning to camp after dark. Leave camp at dawn and head on up the drainage. In 2.5 to 3 miles, a small drainage comes in from creek left (the east). If you go another 1/4 mile, you will reach the main junction of Crystal Creek with Dragon Creek, and will have gone too far. The small side canyon coming in from the east has a pourover about 90 feet high at the junction with Crystal Creek. You will need to climb around this pourover on its northern side. Return to the dry bed of this drainage, which in 1/4 mile or so will turn toward the south and the Tower of Ra. In another 1/4 mile, a small tributary comes in from the east (creek right). Go past that, continuing in the main drainage and heading south 1.25 miles to the saddle between the Tower of Ra and Osiris Temple. Unfortunately, between you and that saddle is the Redwall.

This route gets fairly tight in the Redwall, and will box out at a pour over at one point. From just before this pour over you will need to leave the bed of the drainage and climb up a very steep brushy slope on creek right. Do not reenter the creek, but keep right on going up the slope, finding your way to the top of the Redwall. Once you have topped the Redwall, stay in the Supai and traverse south back into the drainage, then up to the Ra- Osiris saddle. From here, you have two options. If it's getting late, enjoy the view and head back to camp the

Lower Crystal Camp
Upper Crystal Camp

Flow
98

Crystal Creek to Osiris Temple Mile 98.0 R

1/2 Mile

N

VERY DIFFICULT

Osiris Temple

42. Crystal Creek to Osiris Temple contd.

way you have come. If you have enough time and energy, you might want to climb Osiris Temple while you are here. Osiris is only 3/4 mile away.

To climb Osiris, head northeast from the saddle up the ridge toward Osiris. Skirt the west side of the first set of Supai cliffs you come to that you can't easily climb. In about 1/4 mile you will come to a broken section of Supai that allows you access right up to the top of the Supai with some ledge work back and forth. From here it's a 1/2 mile walk east up the west ridge to the top of Osiris.

What a view! With the Tower of Ra just to the west, Horus Temple and the Tower of Set are to the south. To the north is Claude Birdseye Point, and majestic Isis Temple is to the east. It doesn't get any better than this. You are really a long way from camp here. There is water back in Crystal Creek if you have run out by now (not good), and you would be advised to get below the Redwall by dusk, and into Crystal Creek by dark.

43. Bass Camp to Merlin Abyss and Modred Abyss

A fine camp with lots of wonderful hiking makes Bass a very sought-after camp. It is hot here in the summer, but this camp has lots of winter sun. The pull-in for this camp is fairly straightforward. Once you have run Bass Rapid, the river turns left or to the west. Almost at the very end of this turn and tucked into a small eddy is Bass Camp (Mile 108.25 R). This is a very heavily used camp, so please do a good sweep of this camp as you leave, and leave it cleaner than when you arrived.

Hikes from here are many. For a short, easy, hour-long stroll, you can walk back upriver on the flat bench trail just behind camp. In less than 1/4 mile, you will find the north landing for the Bass Cable Crossing. In another 100 yards or so, look for cairns marking a chute leading down through the Schist to the sandy beach at the foot of Bass Rapid. If you look for it, you might find the small inscription from "Geo. W. Parkins Washington DC 1903" chiseled in the rock near the head of the beach. It's as leisurely a walk back to camp as it was to get here.

Another easy hike requiring a little more work is to hike the North Bass Trail into the Shinumo drainage and up to the old Bass Camp. The North Bass Trail is to the northeast behind camp. The trail winds north up 1/2 mile to a small saddle, then drops down 1/2 mile to Shinumo Creek. It's another 1/2 mile up the south side of the creek to the old Bass Camp. There are a lot of odds and ends from the camp under a small overhang. Take only pictures, and leave all this stuff alone.

From here, there is a more challenging and difficult hike farther up the Shinumo drainage. Follow the North Bass Trail another 1/2 mile to the junction of White Creek coming in from the north and Shinumo Creek coming in from the east. Cross to the north side of Shinumo Creek here, and leave the Bass Trail, proceeding east along Shinumo Creek. In another 1/2 mile, there is a break through the Tapeats to the north. Climb up through this difficult break. Once you have gained the top of the Tapeats, it's a 2.5-mile walk along the Tapeats top to the junction of Merlin Abyss and Modred Abyss. Follow the path and avoid stepping on the desert vegetation. Though you can't see them, Holy Grail Temple is just to your west, King Arthur Castle is to the east, and Elaine Castle to the north. This is indeed a fitting haunt for Merlin, should he want to come for a visit. Though there is water along this route, it is very hot here in the summer. You are a long way from camp here, so don't stay long if you want to get back to camp by dark.

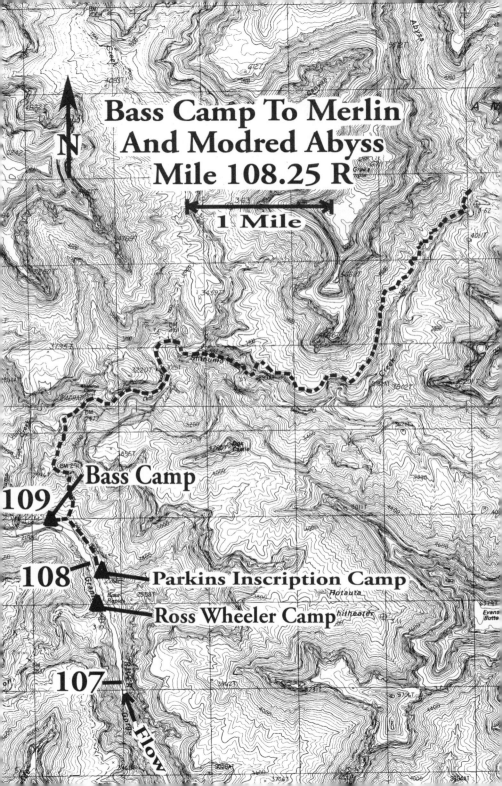

Bass Camp To Merlin
And Modred Abyss
Mile 108.25 R

N

⊢———— 1 Mile ————⊣
1 Mile

Bass Camp

109

108 — **Parkins Inscription Camp**

Ross Wheeler Camp

107

Flow

44. Bass Camp to Fan Island

There are any number of climbs in the Bass area that require a rope. Fan Island, just 1 1/2 miles northwest of camp, has one very difficult move in a chimney right at the top. A good scrambler will not need a rope, but this is a very difficult hike. Others will find this route challenging enough to want a little help from a rope, or to stay at the base of the Redwall. The camp for this hike is described in hike # 43. Please note that this hike is for the most part on south-facing slopes. If it's a hot day, go hang in Shinumo Creek.

From Bass camp, hike west-northwest following the cairn-marked trail to a small saddle only 1/4 mile from camp. Follow this trail back down into Shinumo Creek. Cross the creek, and proceed up the creek another 1/2 mile, staying on the creek-right side. You will encounter a large wash entering the creek from the northwest called Burro Canyon. At this point, follow the ridge to the west of Burro Canyon. The reason to climb this ridge is that there is a rather large pourover in Burro Canyon you will need to avoid. Follow this ridge 1/2 mile up through some broken cliffs to the level of the Tonto and traverse west 1/4 mile, then north 1/4 mile, to the south face of the Fan Island Redwall. This face is the key to this whole hike.

In the middle of this south face, look for a small chute heading up and slightly to the east. Follow this chute up, then head east up behind a bedroom-sized flake of Redwall. Behind this flake, you will find a 4-foot-wide ledge ramping to the east and up slightly. This ledge is the key. If you are out on a 6-inch ledge, you are not in the right place! Take this ramp to its end. From here you will have to turn back to the north on a second exposed ledge back to a ridge on the east corner of the south wall. Cross this ridge and drop down into and cross a small chute. From here, climb up to the base of a 15-foot-high chimney. This is the crux move of this hike, and where a rope could come in handy. Once above this chimney, you are a short walk from the flat top of Fan Island.

The view here is truly Grand. Waltenberg Rapid is visible off to the west. Mount Huethawali is across the river to the south, and Evans Butte is to the southeast, with Dox Castle below and in front of Evans. Holy Grail Temple is to the northeast. You can almost see camp from here as well. Speaking of camp, what goes up must go down. Please use extra caution on the descent through the Redwall.

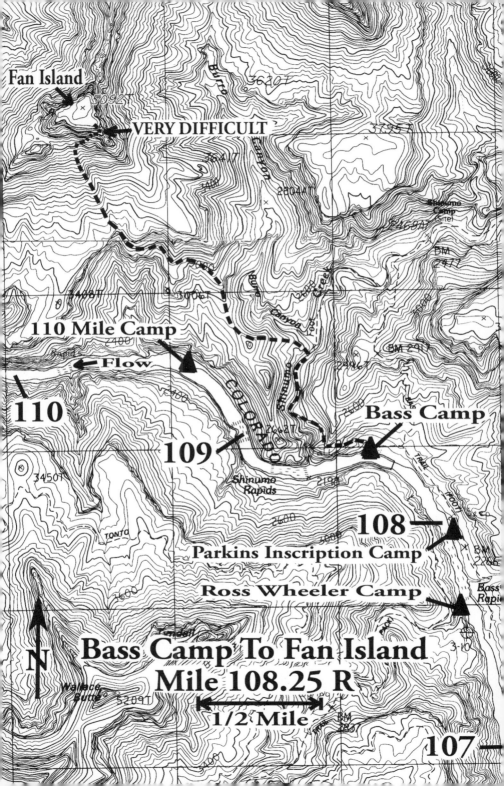

Fan Island

VERY DIFFICULT

110 Mile Camp

← Flow

110

109

Bass Camp

Shinumo Rapids

108 →

Parkins Inscription Camp

Ross Wheeler Camp

Bass Rapi

COLORADO

N

Bass Camp To Fan Island
Mile 108.25 R

1/2 Mile

107

45. Lower Shinumo Creek

Just downstream from Bass Camp, Shinumo Creek reaches the river. There is a great waterfall here, and a short, beautiful, easy walk. Grand Canyon National Park regulations do not allow camping here. Remember, the use of soap in any side stream in the park or within 100 yards of the mouth of side tributaries like Shinumo Creek is not allowed either. This is a great spot for lunch and a dip in Shinumo Creek on a hot summer day. Be ready to share this heavily visited spot with other river runners.

The pull-in here is a bit tricky. Stay close to the right shore. You can pull in at the very top of the Shinumo debris fan (Mile 108.5 R) and walk on down to the creek. You can also float downstream another 100 yards to the mouth of the creek. You have to float away from shore to clear a few rocks, but don't let the current sweep you on downriver. As soon as you see the mouth of the creek, pull on in. If you miss the pull-in, you will be swept on downstream through Shinumo Rapid.

Once you have landed, it's a very short few-hundred-foot wet walk to a 15-foot waterfall in the tight narrows of Shinumo Creek. Unless it is choked by flood debris, look for a chimney up through the boulders on the creek-left side of the back of the waterfall. If you can squeeze through this chimney, you can walk up Shinumo Creek. It's a wonderful riparian creekbed in a dry desert. The return journey can include a jump from the top of the waterfall into the pool below. Make sure the pool is deep enough for this activity on your way up, as on occasion it is full of gravel. All this water fun is just too cold to even think about in the winter months.

110 Mile Camp

Flow

Bung Canyon

Little Creek

BM 2917

2906T

Bass Trail

2600

Waterfall

2662T

109

Shinumo
Rapids

Pull-In

Upper Pull-In

Bass Camp

Trail

108

2600

3000

**Shinumo Creek
Mile 108.5 R**

Trail

N

1/4 Mile

46. Hakatai Canyon

Hakatai Canyon, at Mile 110.7 R, offers a short hike up to some nice schist narrows. These narrows are not narrow enough to be a cool place to avoid the summer heat, but on a cloudy or cool day, you can explore this area up through the schist and Tapeats. Be forewarned the Bass Hakatai Asbestos Mine is up this way, and the mine digs are closed to visitation due to the asbestos dust hazard.

The pull-in can be tricky here. You will want to pull in 100 yards or so above Hakatai Rapid at a small sandy beach. Look for a small trail leading up to the north tramway station for the cable crossing William Bass built across the river here. The tramway landing is identified by a small rock wall on the ridge top above this beach. From here, take the trail down the north side of this ridge to the floor of Hakatai Canyon. Once you reach the canyon floor, head up the tight schist canyon bottom. There are some nice twists and turns in the first 1/2 mile, and in all but the hottest of summers, you'll find water here. In 1/2 mile from the river the tight canyon opens up into a sun-soaked canyon. The route back to the boats is as you have come.

Hakatai Canyon
Mile 110.7 R

N

|← 1/2 Mile →|

Fan
Island

Bass Mine
(no visitation allowed
due to asbestos hazard)

Flow

Hakatai
Rapids

111

110

Fishta
Butte

47. Elves Chasm

On a hot summer day, Elves Chasm is a jewel in the desert. This wonderful side canyon with a small, clear-flowing stream is a very popular stop for many river runners. You will want to cooperate with other trips in managing the limited boat pull-ins at this site. Grand Canyon National Park regulations do not allow camping within 1/4 mile of the mouth of Elves Chasm.

There are three pull-ins for the visit to Elves. The first (Mile 116.25+ L) is less than 1/4 mile above the mouth of the canyon. Look for spots to tie up at some small sand beaches. The second pull-in is just above the point that defines the upper edge of the mouth of Elves Chasm. It's a scramble up over a rocky outcrop and over the rocks down into the chasm. The third pull-in (Mile 116.5 L) is at the very top of the debris fan of the chasm. This pull-in is small, with a tiny eddy for parking the boats. The river sweeps on by into the riffle below.

Regardless of where you park the boats, the easy route up the drainage is on creek right, up against the wall of the drainage. There are a few points where you might want to give each other a hand. The heavy visitation here has polished the travertine rock to a smooth slick surface, so mind your step. In 100 yards, you will find a small waterfall with a pool below it in a deep, narrow, shady canyon.

If you want to continue on up the drainage from here, it can be done, but you will do well to keep the following in mind. To protect the Kanab ambersnail, upper Elves is closed to visitation March through October. If you decide to climb above, there may be fellow river travelers below you, so do not let even small stones become dislodged as you hike over them.

If you must go on this very difficult hike, climb up the Tapeats sandstone on creek left just 100 feet downstream from the pool and waterfall. You will find a small path leading up 100 feet or so. You will then need to traverse along a small ledge back into the drainage. This ledge gets pinched out by a Tapeats tongue, but you can crawl under the tongue and continue another 50 feet on this ledge to a chockstone. There is a chimney here 15 feet or so high. The trick here is in starting the chimney, as it is very wide at its base. From the top of this chimney, the route is across and up the boulders on the other side and into the creekbed again to another pool and waterfall. From here, the route continues on up creek left up a steep cliff of Tapeats Sandstone another 100 feet or more, with help from occasional giant-sized steps. At the top of this section, there is a short walk to another pool, which is passed on creek left as well.

Elves Chasm
Mile 116.5 L

N

1/4 Mile

4727

4601

Aisle

Stephen
Flow

4572T

Explorers
Monument

117

4000

2800

2600

Rapids

116

Elves
Chasm

3200

3400

3200

4200
4000

Creek

Natural
Arc

Spring

4000

44597

2700

**Clear Creek Waterfall
Hike #36**

**19 Mile Route,
Hike #7**

Diamond Peak
Hike #91

Nautiloid Canyon
Hike #15

Stone Creek
Hike #53

Little Nankoweap
Hike #21

**Tanner Canyon
Hike #29**

**Carbon-Chuar Loop
Hike #27**

**The Tabernacle
Hike #33**

Ochoa Point
Hike #30

Phantom Ranch
Hike #37

91 Mile
Hike #38

Bass Camp
Hike #43

Bass Camp
Hike #43

Elves Chasm
Hike #47

Stone Creek
Hike #53

Olo Canyon
Hike #58

Matkatamiba pull-in
Hike #59

Havasu Canyon
Hike #61

Tuckup Canyon
Hike #62

Tuckup Canyon
Hike #62

View of Parashant Camp
Hike #77

Parashant Canyon
Hike #77

47. Elves Chasm contd.

The route goes another 100 feet or so up a small side drainage on creek left here, over a few ledges and into a thick stand of saw grass. There is a small seep here, and the path is very slick, with a 50-foot fall below. Once through the saw grass, the route goes back into the creekbed and crosses the stream once again.

The route now goes up a slick pourover and into the base of another boulder-choked chimney. You will need to climb up over a slippery boulder with a few key handholds. Once above this point, a little more boulder hopping takes you into the last bowl on this journey. There is a trickling waterfall and small pool with boulders scattered about to lounge on. This is indeed a nice quiet place to spend a little time, but if you attempt to climb to this point, please exercise the utmost caution. You should bring a little food and water on this journey.

48. Blacktail Canyon

Blacktail has a wonderful Tapeats narrows. This short and easy walk from the river is a place you must go with those of your group that have musical skills. After spending days out in the wilds, the narrows of Blacktail offer a place of comfort and silence too. There are two camps on river left just above Blacktail (Mile 119.5 L, Mile 119.75 L) and two at the mouth of Blacktail Canyon (Mile 120 R), one at the top of the debris fan and the other on through the riffle and tucked in at the foot of the fan.

The hike is really very short, less than 1/2 mile round trip. From either camp, follow the path leading into the drainage. Walk up the drainage and you will quickly enter a deep Tapeats slot canyon. You will have to climb around or wade through a few pools to reach the chockstone in the back of the narrows. There is a permanent trickle of water here. This is a great place to play some music or sit in silence and contemplate. This is also a highly visited attraction site, so be ready to share your visit with other river parties.

A good climber can climb out the back of Blacktail, past the chockstone and another behind it. This depends not only on the climber's skill though. If the last flashflood through Blacktail has removed all the gravel's below this chockstone, forget it. If you get past this chockstone, there is a car-sized boulder wedged 15 feet overhead that you will walk under before you find a way out of the Tapeats on creek right. There is a path leading back toward the river on top of the Tapeats, and it's easy to make your way down to the debris fan through the broken ledges of Tapeats from here.

Blacktail Canyon
Mile 120.0 R

Conquistador Flow

121

1/4 Mile

N

120.9 Left Camp ▲

Aisle

COLORADO

120.2 Left Camp
(low water) ▲

Lower Blacktail Camp

120 ▲

Blacktail

Opposite Blacktail
Camp ▲▲

Hundred and Twenty Mile Canyon

Upper Blacktail Camp

▲
120 Mile Camp

▲
Shady Grove Camp

119

▲ 119.2 Mile Camp

49. Forster Canyon

There's a long straightaway of river along this stretch called Conquistador Aisle. The Esplanade on the north side of the river has five terraces named for five different Spanish explorers of the Conquistador era, hence the name. At the end of this aisle is a wonderful camp at Mile 122.7 L. This camp can have an awesome sunset view, and it gets early morning sun as well. There's a nice short easy hike from camp the 1 and 1/2 miles you can go up Forster Canyon.

To hike up Forster Canyon, head from camp on the trail leading to the drainage bottom. Once in the drainage bottom, turn left, and off you go. It's easy going up the drainage bottom, but keep in mind that you are at the base of the Redwall, with no way out of this drainage. After a little over a mile, the drainage twists and turns a little, then forks. Both of these forks end in impressive Redwall pourovers. There is full-on sun in here at midday, but nice shade in the early morning and late afternoon. The return is as you have come.

Since we are mid-book more or less, now is a good spot to refer back to the introductory section of the book. Maybe it's time to refresh our memory about all of the things that are fragile in this place—all of the things that are depending on us treading lightly as we pass through this wonderful canyon. From the fragile soils to the fragile shrubs and plants to the fragile archaeological ruins, all are depending on us to safeguard and protect them. If we don't mind where we are going, who will? Also, in another 10 to 15 miles down-canyon, the river might get a little crowded, as a lot of trips will want to stop at Tapeats Creek and Deer Creek. Don't forget to ask the other trips you encounter about what they are planning on doing. Coordinate and cooperate with others as much as you can so that everyone has a fine Canyon journey. Finally, keep on keeping a clean camp.

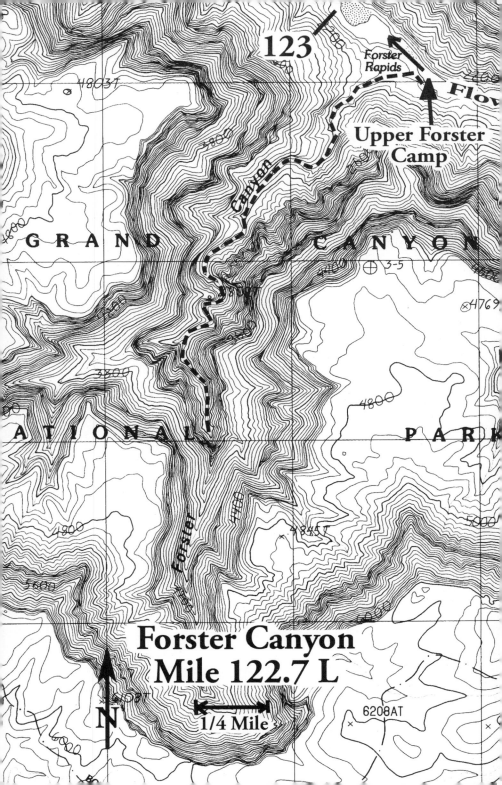

123

Forster
Rapids

Flo

**Upper Forster
Camp**

Canyon

48031

GRAND

CANYON

3-5

4769

3800

4800

ATIONAL

PARK

5000

4800

4845

Forster

4800

4800

5000

4800

5600

Forster Canyon
Mile 122.7 L

N

1/4 Mile

6208AT

6208AT

50. 123.5 Mile Route

Getting through the Redwall on river left in this general area of the Canyon is not easy. There is a fine easy route out the South Bass Trail 15 miles back upriver, and a hairball route just below Elves Chasm 6 miles back. Downriver, you won't see a route this easy past the 123.5 Mile Route till Matkatamiba Canyon 22 miles downriver. The difficult hike to the Redwall top here will take you a good two hours and is steep with some scrambling, but the view from the top is well worth the effort.

The pull-in for this hike is on river left at Mile 123.5. As soon as you run Forster Rapid, look downstream. In the Redwall cliffs on river left, you will see a large chute running up through the Redwall, going parallel to the river as it goes up. The pull-in is where the small drainage coming from the base of this chute reaches the river. Tie up here, and head up this drainage about 1/4 mile. In the lowest bands of overhanging burnt orange Muav cliffs on creek left you will pass a small Ancestral Puebloan dwelling. Just above this spot is a pourover you will need to bypass on the creek-left side.

As you approach the base of the chute, you will see another chute going up in the same direction as the main one. You need to turn here and head up this smaller steep chute a few hundred yards, to the northwest. Just before you reach a small saddle at the top of this chute, turn back to the south along a bench that leaves the chute you are in and goes around the corner out of sight toward the main chute. Following this bench will lead you back into the main chute above an impressive waterfall. From here it's a scramble up the main chute, with only a few small pourovers to work past before you reach the top of the Redwall. A 1/4 mile hike south along the rim will take you to a wonderful overlook of Forster Rapid just below you. Mount Huethawali is 10 miles distant to the southeast. From here you can't quite see Fossil Rapid, but to the northeast 10 miles or so is Steamboat Mountain, rising above Deubendorff Rapid. This is Grand Canyon river hiking at its best. Short, steep, and to the point. The route to the boats is as you came. Don't forget to bring along some water and salty snack foods.

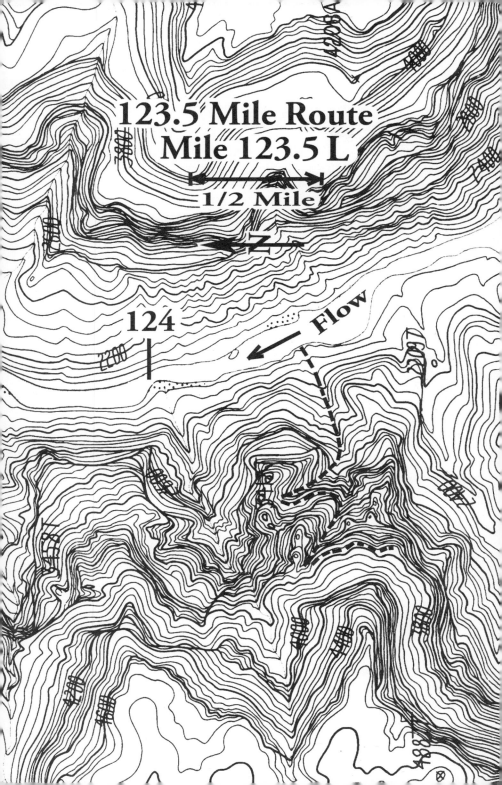

123.5 Mile Route
Mile 123.5 L

1/2 Mile

124

Flow

51. Fossil Canyon

Fossil Canyon is a wonderful easy hike in a drainage few people find the time to explore. There is good camping here too. The main Fossil Camp is just above Fossil Rapid at 124.8 L. The pull-in is a little tricky so stay close to shore here. The next camp downriver, Below Fossil Camp, is just below the last tail waves of the long run out of Fossil Rapid, at Mile 125.4 L. There is a large living-room-sized boulder at the upper end of the Below Fossil Camp, with Tapeats Sandstone ledges running along the back wall of the sandy camp. Both camps have early morning summer shade and some winter sun before noon.

The hike from Below Fossil Camp requires a walk back upriver 1/2 mile. Once you reach the Fossil Canyon wash, head up it for an easy walk another 3/4 of a mile or so to a fork with a tributary entering from the west. There are signs of a massive debris landslide here, with boulders perched on mud pillars. This formation is similar to one 50 miles downriver called Red Slide, which you will see on river right a few miles above Lava Falls. If you hike up this steep west tributary 1/4 of a mile, you can get almost through the Redwall. Alas, the last 200 feet of conglomerate cliff at the top of this tributary kept this ropeless day hiker at bay.

If you hike another 3/4 mile on up the main canyon, you will come to some tight Redwall narrows, with a wonderful ninety-degree dog-leg in them, just like the one in Fossil Rapid. At this point you are tantalizingly close to the top of the Redwall. In the winter, you may be stopped here by a pool of water you will have to swim through in sunless cold narrows if you want to explore this canyon farther. The route back is as you have come.

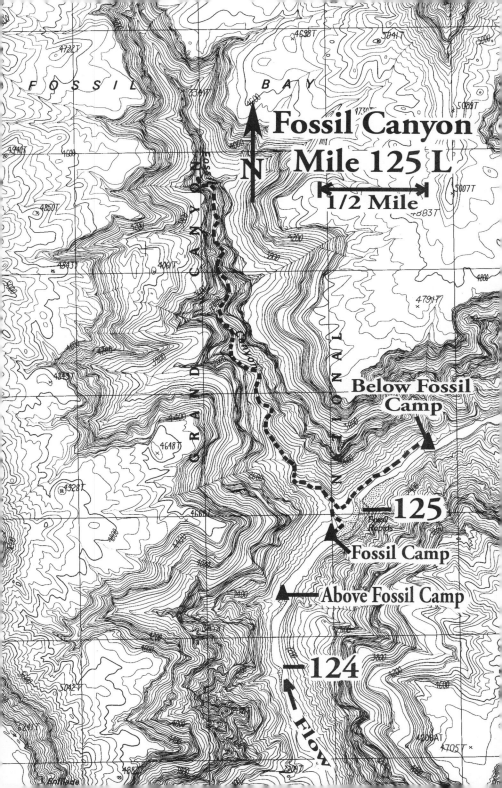

Fossil Canyon
Mile 125 L

N

1/2 Mile

FOSSIL   BAY

GRAND CANYON NATIONAL

Below Fossil
Camp

125

Fossil
Rapids

Fossil Camp

Above Fossil Camp

124

Flow

52. 130 Mile Waterfall

There are a lot of rapids in this reach of the river, called the Middle Granite Gorge. The schist is back, and with it some large rapids. Specter, Bedrock, and Deubendorff are all in this reach. Wouldn't it be nice if you could stop for a minute, catch your breath, and enjoy, say, a nice restful waterfall. You are in luck!

There's a wonderful waterfall at Mile 130.0 R. It's halfway between Specter and Bedrock, and easy to miss. There's a small sandy beach to pull in at just below the mouth of the unnamed tributary where the waterfall is. There is a small trail leading up to the fall's base. Some river parties will draw drinking water here. If it's a hot summer day, there will be no shade for lunch here. This is an impressively high waterslide more than a waterfall. Either way, standing at its base getting soaked looking up at cascading drops of water is a great way to ease the worries of rapids yet to run right out of your mind. Enjoy.

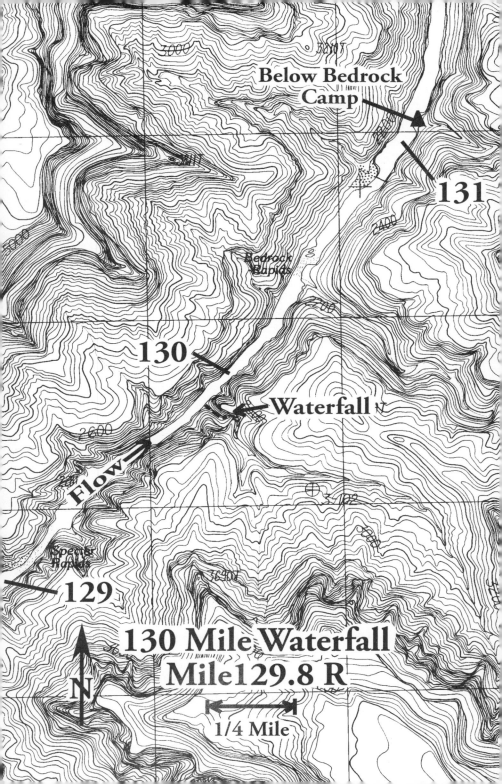

Below Bedrock Camp

131

Bedrock Rapids

130

Waterfall

Flow

129

Spencer Rapids

130 Mile Waterfall
Mile129.8 R

N

|← 1/4 Mile →|

53. Stone Creek and Stone Galloway Loop

Here is another place where there is a lot to do. There used to be a great camp at the foot of Deubendorff Rapid (Mile 132.0 R), but the sand is disappearing at an alarming rate, and you can count on the water dropping out on you in the middle of the night. Where once you had to get your boats back to the water over sand, now you do it over boulders. Not a lot of fun. Still, it's a great place to go exploring. There is a small camp just above Deubendorff Rapid at Mile 131.7 R as well. To hike to the Stone Creek waterfalls from this upper camp, you will need to hike along the shoreline 1/4 mile or less to the mouth of Stone Creek. Stone Creek has recently experienced major monsoon storms and flash floods, washing out most of the vegetation along the streambed.

From the lower camp, hike over the boulder pile to the northeast, following a small pathway leading to the permanent water in Stone Creek. There is an easy walk 1/4 mile or less up this path to a wonderful waterfall that is a great get-wet spot in the heat of summer. This is a common attraction site, so expect to share it with others.

If you want to hike above this waterfall, you will need to hike back less than halfway to the boats and look for a trail up creek left. You climb up through the gray crumbly Diabase Sill volcanics 75 to 100 feet above Stone Creek, then contour along this trail past the wonderful waterfall below. There is a lot of exposure here, so step cautiously. The route continues up Stone Creek, crossing and re-crossing the creek. There are many wonderful spots to stop and hang along the way, but it's worth the walk on this one to go the extra mile (actually 2 miles from the river) to the waterfall in the Tapeats narrows at the end of the trail. There is great shade here in the summer, and fine pools to contemplate. There is a small Ancestral Puebloan dwelling just below the waterfall at trail's end on creek right. It is hidden by thick willow and hard to spot. As with all archaeological sites, don't touch the fragile walls.

Those who want a tougher walk can backtrack 1/4 mile or so from the end of the trail and hike out of the Tapeats narrows on creek left. From here you can climb up-slope a little more to the top of the Tapeats and hike back southwest along the base of Arrowhead Terrace. At the end of the Terrace you turn south and cross over into Galloway Canyon. Continue along the top of the Tapeats until you hike right into the drainage in Galloway. You will have covered a little over 2 miles in full sun, so take extra water when doing this in the summer. From here, hike back the 2 miles down Galloway all the way to the river, turn right and walk down along the river to camp.

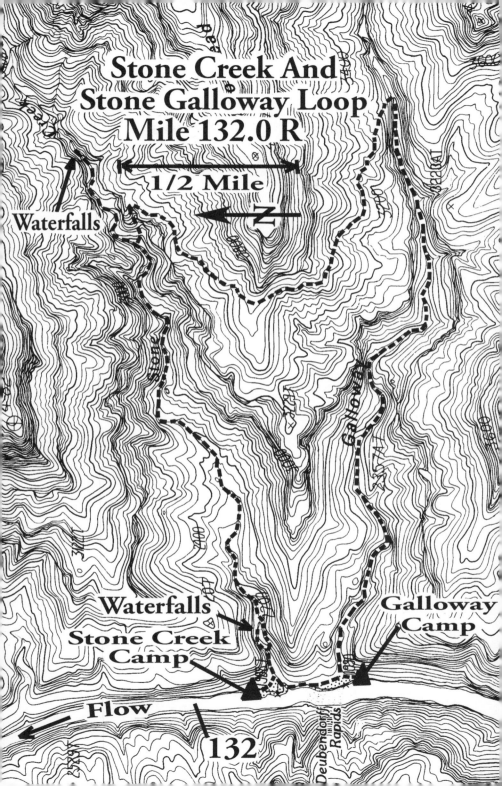

Stone Creek And
Stone Galloway Loop
Mile 132.0 R

1/2 Mile

N

Waterfalls

Stone

Galloway

Waterfalls

Stone Creek
Camp

Galloway
Camp

Flow

132

Deubendorff Rapids

54. Thunder River Deer Creek Loop

Tapeats Creek, with its shade trees and clear cool water, offers an easy walk to many wonderful areas. For the more energetic hiker, a difficult walk up to the magnificent Thunder River Spring, then on across Surprise Valley into the Deer Creek drainage and on to the river offers a great day loop hike.

There is no camping at the mouth of Tapeats Creek (Mile 133.75 R). There is a pull-in just above Tapeats Creek Rapid. Stay close to the cliff at water's edge, and pull in as this cliff retreats into the mouth of Tapeats Creek. This pull-in is small, and as Tapeats Creek is a popular attraction site, you should plan on having other river parties stop in and share this access point. You will need to ford Tapeats Creek to hike from this pull-in. During high runoff in the spring, this can require teamwork and the establishment of a throw bag for a hand line across the creek. There is a camp well below the mouth of Tapeats Creek, at the foot of the rapid at 133.9 R. This camp has a surging eddy with a boulder beach. You will not have to ford Tapeats Creek to start hiking from this camp as the trail up Tapeats Creek starts just upstream of this camp. Other camps to stage for Tapeats are Racetrack, Talking Heads, Stone Creek, Galloway and Below Bedrock. You can hike the 1/8 mile from Racetrack up through the diabsae sill and around into Tapeats if you want to layover at Racetrack, and can stay high and bench around to the creek upstream of the Tapeats narrows.

For a short hike to some deep pools and water slides, hike up creek right 100 yards and then follow the trail 1/4 mile up a chute and onto the top of a high cliff with a good view of camp. From here, it is another 1/4 mile or slightly more back to the creek. There are some fun water slides here; a great place to cool off on a hot summer day.

To continue on to Thunder River, follow the trail another few 100 yards to a ford. The trail crosses Thunder River here to creek left. This crossing can be very difficult in the spring runoff. You can continue on creek right, but the creek right trail has some scrambling and exposure in another 1/2 mile or so. If you cross the creek to creek left, a good trail follows the creek for another 3/4 of a mile, then re-crosses Tapeats Creek and joins the trail following creek right.

From here it's another 1/4 mile to the Tapeats Creek campground used by backpackers, and just beyond that the trail intercepts Thunder River. This is supposed to be the only place in the lower 48 states where a river empties into a creek. The trail turns up the river-right side of Thunder River at this point and climbs another 3/4 of a mile to the cool shade trees at Thunder River Springs. This is a great place to have that lunch you packed and cool off.

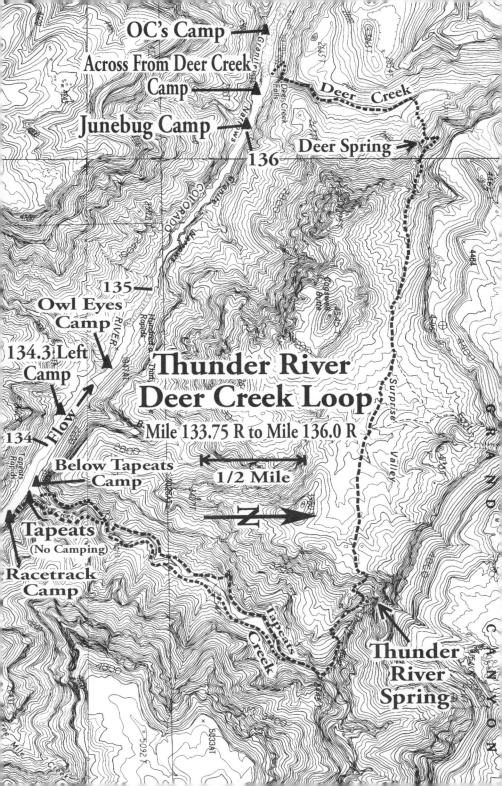

OC's Camp

Across From Deer Creek
Camp

Junebug Camp

136

Deer Creek

Deer Spring

135

Owl Eyes
Camp

134.3 Left
Camp

134

Flow

Below Tapeats
Camp

Tapeats
(No Camping)

Racetrack
Camp

Thunder River
Deer Creek Loop

Mile 133.75 R to Mile 136.0 R

1/2 Mile

N

Tapeats Creek

Surprise Valley

Thunder
River
Spring

54. Thunder River Deer Creek Loop contd.

Once you have hydrated and cooled down from the steep hike up to the spring, the next stretch of this trail is across the shadeless Surprise Valley and into the Deer Creek drainage. In the summertime, this will be hot, so get your shirt wet at the spring before you head out toward Deer Creek. The trail climbs under 1/2 mile to the flat table-land of the Surprise Valley, and in another 3/4 of a mile intercepts the Bill Hall Trail, coming in from the north. Continue on west another 1 1/2 miles, past Cogswell Butte to the south and into the Deer Creek drainage. The trail starts its descent about 1/2 mile past the Bill Hall junction. In another mile or so the trail winds into a small side canyon of the Deer Creek drainage and passes Deer Spring.

In the heat, it's worth the 100-yard walk over to this great spring to get wet and cool off. There is deep, cool shade on the creek-left side of the spring, with a little scramble up 50 feet of slope to reach the Throne Room. Someone has strategically placed a few slabs of limestone here into some wonderful seats with a majestic view! From Deer Spring, continue your descent another 1/4 mile to the floor of the Deer Creek valley. Once at the valley floor, the trail fords the small brook in Deer Creek, then heads down-valley on creek right for about 1/2 mile to the Deer Creek Patio, as the top end of the Deer Creek narrows is called. Just 100 feet above the patio is a wonderful 5-foot waterfall into a pool of water. As they say, "If you're hot, you're stupid." This is a good place to get wet on a hot summer day before you begin the last leg back to the river.

It's less than 1/2 mile from here to the river, but there is one last obsta-cle to pass, the Deer Creek narrows. Just a few hundred yards from the patio, the otherwise wide trail turns into a narrow ledge with a drop into the roaring waters of Deer Creek below. Look for Puebloen hand prints here, just before a 40-foot section of ledge which at one point is about 1 foot wide. Once you pass this difficult spot, the trail continues on another 200 yards or so to a fine view. The mouth of Deer Creek and the Colorado River are just below you and the Powell Plateau makes up the southeastern skyline, while Fishtail Point is visible to the northwest. From here the trail continues a little over 1/4 mile to the Colorado River at the base of the impressive Deer Creek Falls. You will be passing by a small patch of poison ivy, so stay on the trail. So where are the boats? Hopefully, you have left some of your party at Tapeats Creek to ferry the boats the 2.5 miles from there to Deer Creek. By this time you would be right in thinking to head on downriver and look for camp. Fortunately, there are five great camps all on river left in the next 1/2 mile downriver. Remember, no camping on river right from 1/4 mile above Deer Creek to 1/2 mile below. Enjoy.

55. Deer Creek

Deer Creek, at Mile 136.2 R, is one of those spots in Grand Canyon that is well worth the time to visit. Most river trips will stop here for at least a short time to enjoy the magnificent riverside waterfall. Others will hike up to the Deer Creek Patio, past the Deer Creek narrows, which is not for those with a fear of heights. Still others will hike to Deer Spring (also called Dutton Spring) and enjoy the shade of the Throne Room. There is a lot to do here, so expect to share this Eden with other river parties.

There is no camping allowed from 1/4 mile above to 1/2 mile below Deer Creek ON RIVER RIGHT. That's fine because there are six camps in this same reach on river left. The Deer Creek pull-in is often packed with boats. There is a small bay just 50 yards upstream from the main pull-in, which is often open. There is a difficult scramble up through the schist on the Deer Creek side of this bay, over a small schist ridge, and down to the main pull-in.

From here, it's a few-hundred-foot easy walk to the base of Deer Creek Falls. Those with a desire to blow out their eardrums can try to swim around into the back of the falls.

Those who want to challenge their fear of heights and hike up to the patio at the start of the Deer Creek narrows will want to look for the trail that starts at creek right just below the plunge pool. This well-maintained trail goes up through one of three known locations in Grand Canyon for poison ivy (read stay on the trail) and in a little over 1/4 mile will reach the beginning of the Deer Creek narrows. There is a fine view of the Middle Granite Gorge here, with a great view southeast to the Powell Plateau on the North Rim.

Now for the fun bit. The trail heads into the narrows on a level track, and in a few hundred yards reaches a 40-foot section of 1-foot-wide ledge with a drop to the roaring Deer Creek 75 feet below. Look for Puebloan handprints in this area on the cliff face 3 to 4 feet above the trail. Once past this, it's another few hundred yards to the Deer Creek Patio at the start of the narrows. This is a great place to hang and enjoy the shade. Just up the creek 100 feet or so is a small plunge pool and a great place to cool off.

Some folk may want to bring up a throw bag and drop into the narrows for a little exploration back toward the Colorado River. You will want to cross over to creek left to start this exploration, just above the 20-foot waterfall at the start of the narrows. There is a small ridge of Tapeats just below the falls that you can use to get down into the

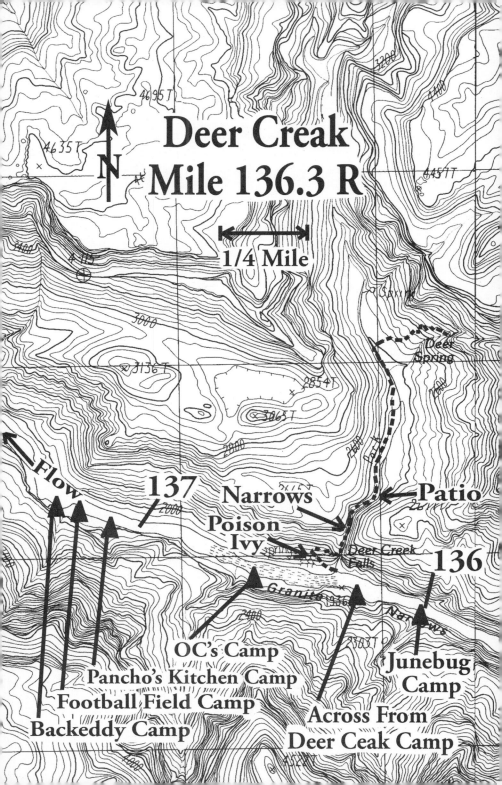

Deer Creak
Mile 136.3 R

1/4 Mile

Deer Spring

Flow

137

Narrows

Patio

Poison Ivy

Deer Creek Falls

136

Granite

OC's Camp

Pancho's Kitchen Camp

Football Field Camp

Junebug Camp

Backeddy Camp

Across From Deer Ceak Camp

55. Deer Creek contd.

start of the narrows. The narrows are a fun place to explore on a hot summer day, but it's too cold to explore here other times of the year. Don't explore here in monsoon season.

Those who want to explore some more might want to hike up the easy trail to Deer Spring. To hike to Deer Spring, head 1/2 mile up the creek-right (west) side of Deer Creek, following the well-worn trail. This trail turns and fords the creek, then climbs 1/4 mile or so up to the spring. Once at the spring, you can climb up the very slippery slope behind the right side of the pour-out to climb up behind the waterfall as it shoots from the solid rock. You can also climb up the 50-foot-high bench on creek left to the Throne Room where someone has strategically placed a few slabs of limestone here to create some wonderful seats with a majestic view. This is a fine place to eat lunch and just sit a spell.

Given a choice, sure, I'd hike to Deer Spring. It's hot up here in the summertime, and there is no safe water to drink until you reach the spring, but hey, this is a hiking book. If some of your party are hiking the up-and-over from Tapeats Creek, you can wait for them at Deer Spring. From here, you hike back the way you came. You will want to bring along some water and food on this hike.

56. 140 Mile Canyon and Keyhole Natural Bridge

This is a place not many folks go. That's fine, because this canyon has a charm all its own. The pull-in for this hike is at the foot of the riffle at the mouth of 140 Mile Canyon (Mile 139.8 L). There is a small camp at the top of the riffle as well. In the mouth of the canyon is a small spring with running water and a few cottonwood trees. It's an enjoyable place to hang out.

To hike to the foot of the bridge, hike on up the drainage. In less than 1/4 mile, you will come to a pourover that has a small trail bypass on creek right, and a very exposed bypass on creek left. There is another pourover just above this one, which is bypassed on creek right. After a little more boulder hopping the canyon floor becomes gravel covered. A half-mile from the river, you will encounter a large side canyon coming in from the west (creek left). To reach the foot of the arch, continue up this western arm another 1/2 mile and work your way through some brush up the slope to the seep and waterfall at the back of this canyon. The little hint of light at the back of this spot way over your head is from the Keyhole Natural Bridge, which you can never get a good view of. Stay in the drainage floor as much as possible to avoid damaging the fragile desert shrubs.

If you stay in the main drainage, there is some very interesting hanging conglomerate about 3/4 mile farther up; then the canyon becomes smooth-floored for a ways. There will be running water in here in the winter. You can explore this drainage another 2 miles from the Keyhole arm, and get tantalizingly close to the top of the Redwall before you reach a 15-foot-high chockstone pourover. It is very difficult to climb around the creek left side of this chockstone. Beyond this, you can only proceed another 1/8 mile or less to a 75-foot-high waterfall cascading down well-polished limestone. It's very gorgeous here. In the summer time, don't even think about hiking here, as this south-southeast trending canyon gets a lot of full-on sun. In the fall, winter and spring, this is interesting country few folks explore, so enjoy.

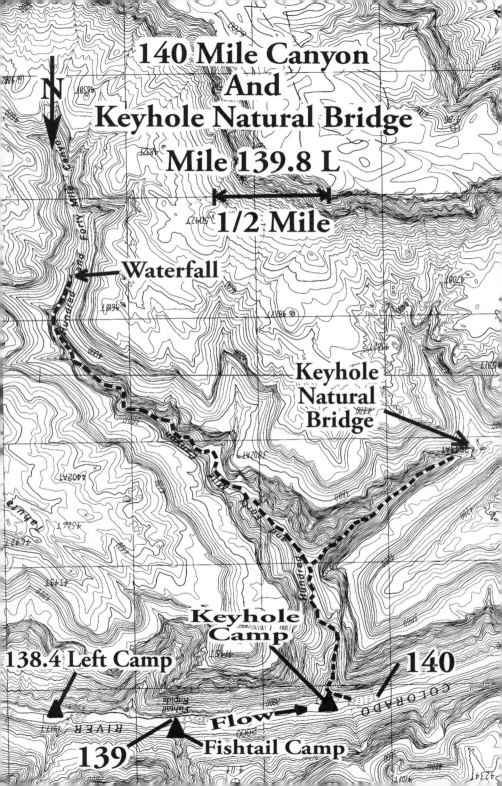

140 Mile Canyon
And
Keyhole Natural Bridge
Mile 139.8 L

1/2 Mile

Waterfall

Keyhole
Natural
Bridge

Keyhole
Camp

138.4 Left Camp

140

139

Flow

Fishtail Camp

N

57. Kanab Creek to Whispering Falls

Kanab Creek doesn't look very inviting at its junction with the Colorado River (Mile 143.5 R). Those who have spent time hiking in Kanab know that its beauty is up-drainage a ways. Kanab Creek offers the hiker deep shade with permanent water in a very narrow, deep limestone canyon if you only take the time to hike up to it. There is a pull-in at the mouth of Kanab Creek (no camping allowed), and the camp marked on river left at Mile 143.25 L is very rough. The best camps are back upriver, from just below Deer Creek 7 miles back to just above 140 Mile riffle 3 miles upriver. Still, there's a small camp downstream of Kanab at 144.2 on river right. You can walk back upriver to Kanab Canyon from this camp.

There's an easy hike to a shady spot just 1/4 mile up the creek. Kanab Creek does not drop very fast, so the walking is easy, though bouldery in places. The creek is very sinuous, with lots of twists and turns. The first good shade is found in a large undercut up the creek a few twists. You will find permanent water up here.

For the more industrious hiker, an easy though tiring walk up 2.5 miles of boulder-hopping creek bottom will bring you to the first side canyon you can easily hike into on creek left. A few hundred yards up this side tributary is a wonderful narrows with an unclimable waterfall. There is a small, heavenly spring here, with water dripping off the waterfall into a fine plunge pool. This spot is known as "Whispering Falls."

Kanab Creek offers shade, though it is a hot canyon in the middle of summer. You will also want to think twice about spending time here during the monsoon season. Heavy rains falling to the north of here anywhere in the extensive Kanab drainage can send floods down the otherwise trickling bed of Kanab Creek. You will want to hike here with enough water and food to last for most of the day.

Whispering
Falls

Kanab Creek to
Whispering Falls
Mile 143.5 R

1/2 Mile

N

Kanab
Point

Kanab

Kanab (No Camping)

Below
Kanab (LW)
Camp

144

Kanab
Rapids

Flow

Above Kanab
Camp

143

58. Olo Canyon

Olo Canyon is a wonderful jewel of a limestone canyon in the heart of the "Muav Gorge," the unofficial name given to this section of the river, between Kanab Creek and Havasu Canyon. The trouble with Olo is getting into it. If you don't have good climbers in your party, you might not want to even stop.

There is a great pull-in at the mouth of the canyon, in the eddy on river left just below the Olo Canyon riffle (Mile 145.7). Unless it's cloudy, there is nice winter lunchtime sun here, but this is a very-low-water camp only. There is also a small camp upstream at Mile 145.1 L, but to camp there you have to be ready to pull in, as you can't see the camp from upstream. One forty-five is a fairly small camp, only 1/4 mile above and an easy walk to Olo. No matter where you start your Olo journey, you only have two very difficult options to enter the canyon. Both require good climbing skills and are best climbed with belay lines.

The first option is at the mouth itself, at the base of a 40-foot pourover. There is often a rope with knots tied in it hanging down in space from an anchor at the top of this pourover. You may last have seen a rope like this in gym class, suspended from the ceiling. You guessed it, just like in gym class, it's a free-climb up a rope with knots for hand holds. Period. There is no cliff close enough to get purchase from, and no place for anyone to help boost you along. Below you is a rock ledge and next to that, a deep pool of water. The real trouble here is at the top of the free-climb. The rope rolls over the rock ledge, and you have to work your hands between the rock and the rope, while your body weight pins your hands between rope and rock. Yes, people have climbed this, and yes, people have fallen from the top and taken a backboard ride to a waiting helicopter from here as well. Once you clear this rope, you are at the base of a small waterfall. Climb out to the creek left side of this waterfall and into the main patio. Funny how this last sentence is so easy to write yet will be almost as difficult to maneuver as the rope you have just come up.

The second option for entering Olo is on the creek-left side of the mouth. Look for a small talus slope leading up to a limestone cliff. Sixty feet up this exposed cliff face is a rock slab, hanging by a song. You need to climb up this cliff and onto the top of the slab, where a small ledge takes you around and into the first patio.

This patio is a wonderful limestone-floored shady spot to catch your breath and wits. You will need them. Your next move is to climb the cone-shaped waterfall at the back of this patio. Approach the waterfall from the creek-right side, avoiding the deep pool of water at the

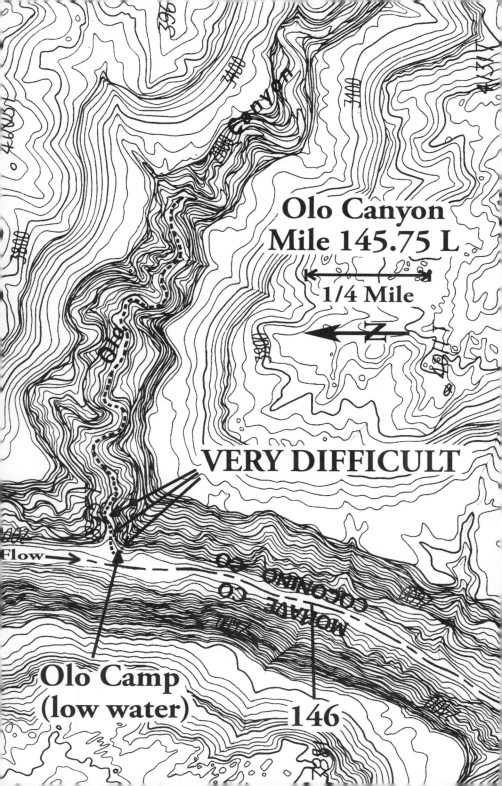

Olo Canyon
Mile 145.75 L

1/4 Mile

N

VERY DIFFICULT

Flow →

MOJAVE CO
COCONINO CO

Olo Camp
(low water)

146

58. Olo Canyon contd.

base of the cone. You will need to get up onto the ledge just to the side of the cone. Imagine climbing onto the top of a large steel file cabinet and you get the picture. From here, you will need to feel around for hand holds at the top of the cone and back behind it. When you are ready, you will have to climb right up the cone, through the water trickling over the edge and making the cone rather slippery. Once up, you can set a rope for the folks below from an old piton hammered into a crack in the rock on creek right.

From here, stay on the creek-left side of the stream and head up away from the creekbed to avoid the pools of water below for another 100 yards. Eventually you end up back in the creekbed. This narrow slot of polished limestone is fun to negotiate and a challenge to stay dry in if you visit on a cold winter day. It is exotic in the summer heat. Another couple of hundred yards of limestone slot canyon leads you to a wonderfully large plunge pool. You can skirt this pool to creek left and enter into an open grove of ash and cottonwood. Beyond this grove is a dry, boulder-hopping good time for another 1/4 to 1/2 mile.

I have never had time enough to keep exploring, but there are often big horn sheep in here. How they get here is a good question. The return journey to the boats is as you came. Think about it. If you have a harder time climbing down something than up it, don't forget to add this to your considerations when thinking about exploring this side canyon. Do be careful.

59. Matkatamiba Canyon to Mt. Akaba

If you want to explore a narrow limestone canyon with permanent water near its mouth, then stop at Matkatamiba Canyon, or "Matkat," at Mile 148.0 L. There is something for everyone here, with an easy walk to the Matkat Patio, a difficult hike to the east arm of Matkat, and a very difficult hike to the summit of Mount Akaba.

There are four access points from the river into Matkat. The first is from a small beach at Mile 147.75 L. Tie up here and hike up-slope on the small path that benches around the 1/4 mile into Matkatamiba Canyon. There is a small trail close to the edge of a Muav cliff. Stay on this level all the way into Matkat till the canyon floor comes up to your level at the Matkat Patio. The second access point is a small, tight eddy at the mouth of Matkat, and if another river party has made the pull-in, don't even try to stop. You can see if anyone is there by eddying out at the dripping spring on river right at Mile 147.75+ R and walking downstream a short way to look into the mouth. If the coast is clear, you will need to have one boat at a time attempt the pull-in. There are tie points for your bowlines in the rock walls at the mouth, but you have to search for them. NPS regulations do not allow camping in the canyon mouth.

From the eddy, it's a fun scramble for 1/4 mile up very tight narrows and through pools of water to an open area called the Matkat Patio. Those who do not want to attempt the chimney moves required to hike up the narrows should look for a small trail climbing up the creek left side of the canyon less than 100 yards from the river. This trail ascends a few hundred feet, and then forks. Turn left and head into Matkat Canyon. If you turn right, you will run into the folk who are hiking into Matkat from downstream. Once you leave this junction, the trail stays on the level and contours back to the Matkat Patio.

If you miss the pull-in and get swept on downstream through Matkatamiba Rapid, don't panic. The third access point to Matkat is on river left just after the tailwaves of Matkatamiba Rapid. Look for the first boulder bar on river left below the canyon mouth. Tie up at this bar and climb up the stair step Muav cliff at this point to intersect the small path coming back upriver from the camp below. Hike up river around into Matkat. The fourth access point is from a small camp at Mile 148.4 L, 1/2 mile below the rapid. To hike back to Matkat from here, you will need to hike downstream just 100 yards or so from this camp. Look for a small ramp of limestone going back and up thirty feet through the band of cliffs you are hiking at the base of. With some giant-sized steps in it, this ramp leads you to the top of this band of cliffs. From here you need to hike up-slope a few hundred yards and then back upriver 1/4 mile, along the top of a 200-foot-high band of

Matkatamiba Canyon to Mt. Akaba Mile 147.9 L

Mount Akaba **VERY DIFFICULT**

1/2 Mile

N

Panameta

Chikapanagi

Opposite Matkat Camp

Matkatamiba

Canyon

148

Matkat Hotel Camp
(small low water)

Below Matkat Camp
(small low water)

Flow

cliffs. This route contours around into the mouth of Matkat. Stay high and you will intercept the trail coming up out of the mouth of Matkat. Follow this level trail into Matkat, and within 1/4 mile you will reach the Matkat Patio.

Folks may want to stay right here. Why ruin a good thing? Others with water and some snack food will want to keep on heading up the canyon. In another 1/4 mile, you will reach a boulder-strewn section of the canyon floor you have to pick your way through. In another 1/4 mile, the water will stop flowing and you will encounter a worse boulder pile than the last one. This pile of garage-sized boulders is best climbed through on creek right. The going gets a lot easier after this, and less than 1/4 mile past this point you reach the junction of the east and south arms of Matkat. To explore the east arm, turn left and head up the often boulder-choked streambed. In another mile, the streambed forks, with the Chikapanagi arm to your left and Panameta arm to your right. Both of these arms cliff out within 1/4 mile of this junction, tantalizingly close to the top of the Redwall. This is a hot place in the summer with no water. To hike to Mount Akaba, stay in the main or south arm of Matkat. In another 3/4 mile, you will get to within a stone's throw of the top of the Redwall and encounter a chockstone. If Matkat has flashed recently with a lot of gravels, the plunge pool below this stone will be full of sand, and you will need to free-climb the 6 feet or so around the creek left side of this stone. If the pool below the chockstone has been flushed out, then getting up past this part is nearly impossible.

If you manage to get past this chockstone, then in less than 1/4 mile you will be able to leave the creekbed and head up 100 yards of sloping chute on creek right to the top of the Redwall. From here, head down-creek less than 1/4 mile and up into the Supai, looking for a broken route to the top of the Supai. You will need to bench back and forth a bit in this area. In roughly 1/2 mile from the bed of Matkat you will top out on the Esplanade, with the top of Mount Akaba in view only a mile away to the east. Hike straight for Akaba, and climb the steep western slope, traversing around to the north side of this east-west running fin. About midway along the north side of this fin there is a chute-and-fault system that allows up-climbing through the Coconino. You will need to bench back west a little in the crumbling Toroweap to the top of the fin. The summit is on the east end of the fin, and there is a climb of 10 feet's worth of cliff to the top. There is a fantastic view of Mount Sinyala to the west on the Esplanade, with Paya Point a mile to the southeast and the Kanab Creek drainage to the north. You are a very long way from the river here; bring a lot of water and a lunch for this hike. In the heat of summer, dream about this hike from the shade of the Matkat Patio.

60. Canyon of a Thousand Names

Canyon of a Thousand Names is actually an unnamed side canyon at Mile 155.5 R. Folks call it Slimy Tick Canyon, Canyon of a Thousand Names, Pete's Pocket, or Jack's Canyon. No matter the name, this small side canyon has a difficult hike to a small waterfall less than 1/2 mile from the river. The trick to exploring here is all in the pull-in.

As you pass the rock in the middle of the river at Mile 154.9, sit up and pay attention. The river turns to the left, with a small waterfall tumbling over a Muav Limestone cliff. You need to pull in above this waterfall by 200 yards, where a small ramp of sand and rock leads down to the river from the ledges above. There's not a lot of room to tie up a lot of boats here. From this point, you can climb up onto the limestone ledges. Look for a path that heads downstream. Avoid multiple trailing here. This path will lead you to the top of the cliff over which the water is cascading before landing in the river below.

From here, proceed up the drainage 50 yards and look for the path heading up away from the drainage bottom on creek right. You will need to proceed up a steep, wet salt slope 100 feet or so. Look for the path traversing level back into the canyon bottom. This is it. You can hike around here and seek shade in the summer, though this south-facing canyon will not have a generous amount of that.

Please mind the native vegetation here. Also remember that the use of soaps in side tributaries is not allowed. Yes, you can proceed farther up into this canyon. It's just that far side of very difficult to proceed up the salt slope on creek left a couple of hundred feet, then traverse along a small wet ledge back into the drainage via a short ramp. But you can't get through the Redwall up the ramp to the west without a rope and climbing gear. Best is to stay in the shade and enjoy Paradise. The route back to the boats is as you have come.

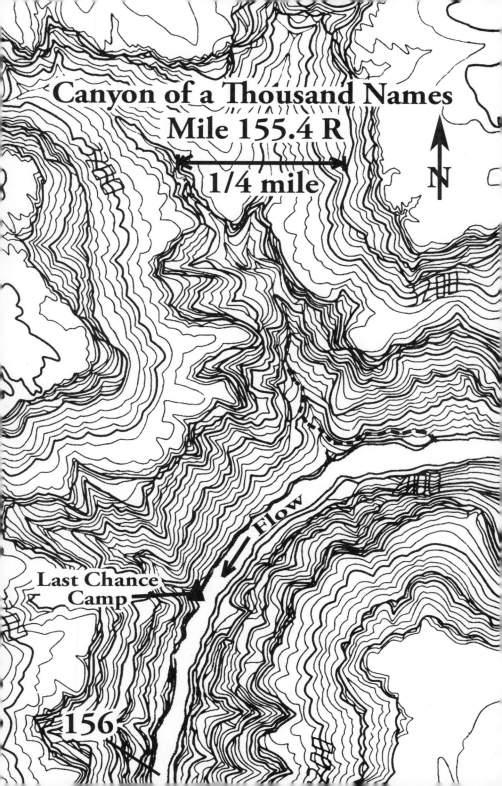

Canyon of a Thousand Names
Mile 155.4 R

1/4 mile

N

Flow

Last Chance
Camp

156

61. Havasu Canyon to Beaver and Mooney Falls

Havasu Canyon is a very heavenly side canyon. Blue waters in the creek and offers of cool shade from the summertime sun await those willing to hike an easy 1/2 mile. Three miles up Havasu is Beaver Falls, while if you hike a little over 6 miles, you will reach the impressive Mooney Falls. Another 2.5 miles above Mooney Falls is the village of Supai, with a telephone and small restaurant. In the winter, Havasu is a cold canyon, with multiple water crossings and little sun.

Because of Havasu's summertime charms and easy hiking, this attraction site is very heavily visited then. Rare is the commercial river trip that will pass without stopping. Be ready to share the pull-in with other trips. Havasu is also a great place to communicate your plans for camp, how long you may be staying in the limited parking at the mouth, and to make more river friends. Unlike most of the other hikes in this book, Havasu is a great stop in the summer, but you might want to row on by in the cold winter months.

In the 9 river miles between Matkatamiba Canyon and the mouth of Havasu Canyon, there are five large camps. All are great camps to stage for an exploration of Havasu. Though "Ledges" and "Last Chance" are the two most often camped at, two more small camps are "Upper Ledges" at 151.25 right and "Sinyella" at 153.75 right. The National Park Service does not allow camping in the mouth of Havasu itself. From any of these camps, access to Havasu is the same. Havasu Canyon enters the main stem at 156.75+ on river left.

You will need to be ready to pull hard into the mouth of Havasu, so be ready to float along the left shore cliffs just above the mouth. There is a small eddy 75 yards or so above the mouth that forces you out into the current a little ways, where the current picks up speed and heads past the mouth. There is also a small piece of Muav jutting out from the left bank cliff a few feet above the mouth. If you attempt to pull in too soon, you can hit this rock and be bounced back into the main current.

Depending on the flow level of the Colorado and whether or not Havasu has recently flashflooded, depositing a lot of gravel in the mouth, the pull-in may be difficult or easy. Anticipate a tight fast eddy, and be ready to pull hard into the mouth once you catch this eddy. If you don't make the pull-in, head on downriver through Havasu Rapid, staying in the chute up against the cliffs on river left. Once below the rapid, look for shade and get ready to hang for the day awaiting the rest of your party.

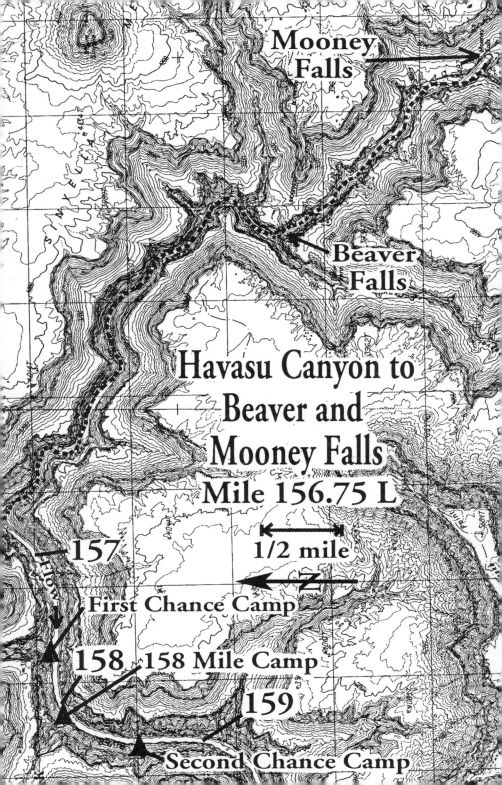

Mooney
Falls

Beaver
Falls

Havasu Canyon to
Beaver and
Mooney Falls
Mile 156.75 L

157

1/2 mile

First Chance Camp

158 158 Mile Camp

159

Second Chance Camp

61. Havasu Canyon to Beaver and Mooney Falls contd.

Once into the mouth of Havasu, move your boats back as far into the mouth as possible, looking for anchors on the walls on which to tie off. This is common courtesy for the next group behind you. If you tie off on other boats, please recognize that they may be leaving before you, and you should leave at least one person at the mouth to assist as "Harbor Master." It should also be obvious that you are parked in the mouth of a tight slot canyon, prone to flashflooding, so in the monsoon season, you will need to be aware of changing weather conditions.

To hike from the boats in the mouth of Havasu, you will need to walk along the ledges leading downstream along the shore of the Colorado. In 100 feet, there is a small ledge with a broken climb up through the Muav. Look for polished limestone where many footsteps have worn a smooth path. This is the start of the Havasu Trail. The trail goes up and back along a ledge above the boats below, heading into Havasu Canyon. In less than 1/4 mile you will reach the first of many creek crossings. The trail crosses from creek left to creek right above a small waterfall. Exercise caution in this crossing, which is hip-deep in fast-moving water. Please note that Havasu Canyon is prone to severe flashflooding, and the following route description may be drastically changed if you visit after the next big flood.

From here, the trail proceeds along the base of broken Muav cliffs on creek right, and in less than 1/4 mile, drops back into the creek. There are a few nice pools to swim in here, ample shade among ledges and an occasional flood-surviving Ash tree. If you would like to proceed on to Beaver Falls, wade along the creek right shore 40 feet or so, and climb away from the creek into a 75-foot section of travertine tunnel, big enough to easily stand up in. There is a rough-hewn chicken ladder aiding your exit from the other end of this tunnel. Follow this path, and in the next 11/2 miles you will cross to creek left, back to creek right, and back to creek left again.

Roughly 2 1/2 miles from the river, the canyon turns from heading roughly southeast to southwest. You are only 1/2 mile from Beaver Falls at this bend in the canyon. The trail re-crosses to creek right and then back to creek left in less than 1/4 mile. At this point, there is a crossing again to creek right at the base of a Muav cliff. If you want to go to Mooney Falls, you will need to look for this crossing, and climb up into this cliff. If you want to go to Beaver Falls, continue on up the creekbed to your last crossing at the foot of Beaver Falls, more a series of travertine plunges than a spectacular waterfall. There is nice shade here as well.

140

61. Havasu Canyon to Beaver and Mooney Falls contd.

To continue on to Mooney Falls, you will need to climb up a chute in the Muav cliff on creek right, below Beaver Falls. At the top of this chute, the trail traverses back along the top of a high bench above Beaver Falls. You are leaving Grand Canyon National Park and entering Havasupai Nation land at this point and need a permit from the Havasupai Tribe. In less than 1/2 mile from leaving the creekbed, the trail drops steeply back into the creekbed above Beaver Falls. There is some serious multiple trailing here, and getting off-trail is very easy. The trail re-crosses the creek three more times before reaching Mooney Falls. Just before the trail reaches the 100-foot-plus-high waterfall, the route is on a high bench on creek left.

If you are going to hike the 2.5 miles from here to the village of Supai, you will need to look for the trail heading up into the wall of travertine on the creek-left side of Mooney Falls. There are more tunnels here, called the Cool Tubes, with chains bolted to the walls to use as handholds along the way. There is some exposure on slippery polished travertine at the top of the tubes. A very well-defined trail leads along creek left past Havasu Falls, then crosses to creek right for the final 2 miles to the village of Supai. There is a small restaurant in the village center, with a pay phone across the street. You may be asked to pick up a day-use permit at the Havasupai Cultural Center, just the other side of the heliport from the restaurant.

The hike from the mouth of Havasu to Beaver Falls and back takes a good three hours. If you want to spend some time there swimming and lounging, add another hour. If you intend to reach the village of Supai, allow at least seven to eight hours for the round-trip hike. The hike to Mooney Falls and Supai can easily be an exercise in multiple trail frustration and take a lot longer than the above mentioned times, as the trail constantly changes due to flood damage.

You will want to carry enough food and water for a full day's hike, though drinking water is usually available at the campground just above Mooney Falls. You will not want to drink the Havasu Canyon water if you can at all help it, even with treatment, due to its high mineral content. The upper reaches of Havasu, especially above Mooney Falls, are sun-drenched and very hot in the summertime.

62. Tuckup Canyon Wanderings

If Havasu is jam-packed with folks and you want to explore a side canyon without a ton of other people, consider Tuckup. The camp here is on river right, at the lower end of the eddy just below Tuckup Rapid at Mile164.5 R. In the winter, this camp gets an hour or so of direct sunlight, and those who stay in camp while you explore the canyon will enjoy the sun. Though difficult to get into, Tuckup contains some amazing country for exploration.

To explore the Tuckup drainage, you will need a throw bag and climbing chock. Hike up the drainage from camp. Within 1/4 mile you will encounter a landslide that has formed a natural dam across this tight limestone canyon. Climb up the creek left side of this pile of rock. You may need to remove your boots to cross the mud flats on the other side. Within another 50 yards or so you will pass a small crack system on your left (that's the west side of the canyon, creek right) that cuts up and back behind you. There is a small chockstone in the bed of the Canyon. Turn around and take a look at that crack. The way up is here. An agile climber can scale up this crack 20 feet to a small ledge. This ledge leads back up-canyon 40 feet to a small chute coming down from above. Your climbing friend will need to climb up this chute another 40 feet to where a large crack on the south side of the chute allows placement of a chock for a fixed rope to be lowered to the less agile below. Using the fixed rope, folk can hand-over-hand their way up this chute. From here, the route continues up the steep chute another 50 feet and then traverses north along a level route a few hundred yards right back to the canyon floor.

There is usually water here, and in the summer, this is an enjoyable hangout. But the adventure has just begun. To keep exploring, continue up the canyon. In another 300 yards look for a route climbing up the side of creek right. The up-climb takes you about 100 feet above the canyon floor, and then traverses another 1/4 mile or less back to the canyon floor.

For another 1/4 to 1/2 mile, the route is up the canyon bottom. Just before you reach the fork between the east and west arms of Tuckup, you must climb over yet another chockstone. If the last flash flood was mostly gravel and little water, you will be able to walk across a gravel-filled plunge pool and climb up the chockstone. If the last flood was mostly water, you will have to swim this pool if you are not a good spider and can't glue yourself to the wall on creek left around this pool. Another few hundred feet beyond this chockstone is the confluence of the two arms. The east arm is the smaller of the two, and it's possible to walk right past it without noticing its entrance into the larger west arm. At this point, you are only about 1 1/2 miles from the river.

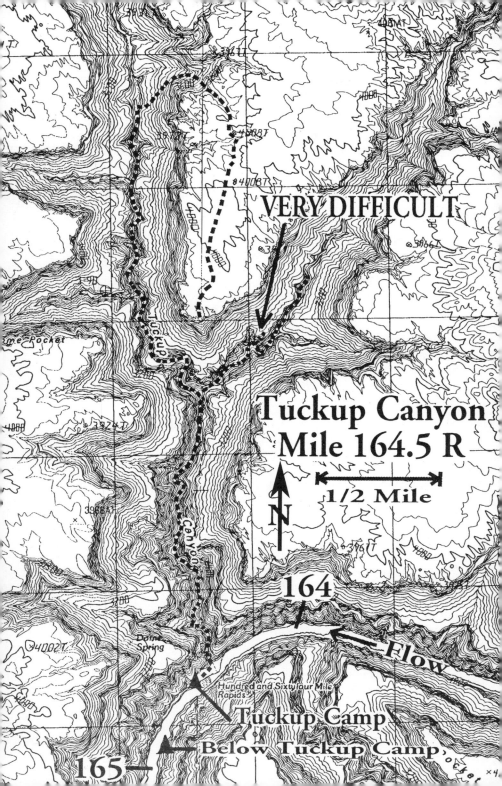

VERY DIFFICULT

Tuckup Canyon
Mile 164.5 R

1/2 Mile

N

164

Flow

Dome Spring

Hundred and Sixtyfour Mile Rapids

Tuckup Camp

Below Tuckup Camp

165

62. Tuckup Canyon Wanderings contd.

The east arm can be explored for another 11/2 miles. About 1/4 mile up the east arm the canyon floor makes a tight gooseneck. In the creek-right bend of this gooseneck, a very difficult route to the top of the Redwall presents itself for the free-climber with good climbing skills. The exposure up this route is extreme. This route goes up the ridge at the corner of the bend to the base of a solid cliff of Redwall. From this point a few hundred feet above the canyon floor, the route then follows a ledge back down-canyon around the base of this cliff and under a slab that has peeled away from the wall and blocks the ledge. Just past this slab there is an easy walk up a chute going back upstream to the Redwall top. Unfortunately, the entrance to this chute is a 10-foot-high cliff with few handholds. The view from the top is of sheer Supai cliffs in every direction.

Those not interested in being a human fly will want to stay in the creekbed and continue beyond this point another 1/4 mile to a small tributary coming in on creek left. There is a nice grotto at the base of an impressively high dry waterfall 1/3 mile up this drainage. Meanwhile, those who continue on up the main east drainage will find a huge chockstone blocking their way. Exploring under this stone reveals a passage up behind the creek-left side of the chockstone. From here, you can continue for another mile, past small chockstones and through a tight limestone canyon to a small unclimbable waterfall.

The west arm of Tuckup is another adventure altogether. A 1/2 mile above the confluence of the east and west arms is an arch of river cobble that the canyon wash has cut beneath. This fragile conglomerate arch is just downstream from a pile of garden shed-sized boulders that can be free-climbed on creek left, or climbed through a passageway in the rubble pile if not filled with debris. From here it's relatively easy going.

About a mile short of Cottonwood Canyon, a route out the creek-left limestone is found in a small drainage with a bowl cut in the very last 50 feet of Redwall. This is a difficult free-climb, with minimal exposure. From here, you can climb up to the base of the Supai. Proceed north along the Supai and around the corner into a small draw coming in from the east. A clear chute leading up into the Supai will become evident. Climb up this chute, which is in the first side drainage coming in from the south. A little scrambling will bring you to the top of the Supai. Walk over the gentle Esplanade a bit south for a mile to a point with a fantastic view of the Tuckup drainage below. The Dome is dominating the western skyline. You are a long way from the boats here, so don't tarry long. In the summer, folks with brains will stay close to the Colorado in the shade of the deep canyon by the pools.

144

63. National Canyon

National Canyon (Mile 166.5 L) is a large drainage that can be hiked 20 miles all the way to the rim. There are two nice camps, both on river left. The upper one is at the sandy beach across from the upper third of the National riffle, while the lower one is at the eddy at the foot of the riffle. Be aware, the sun does not shine here in the winter.

The hikes here are easy to very difficult, depending on how far up the drainage you go. All hikes start up the canyon behind either camp. The wide wash at the start of this hike quickly narrows down into a deep limestone canyon with towering cliffs on both sides. A little over 1/4 mile up, you will need to hike over a small rock-fall dam, less than half the size of the one in Tuckup. There is a nice limestone patio here, with running water and deep shade in the summer. In 1/2 mile or so from the river, the drainage gets very narrow at a small twisting water-fall, with an unclimbable waterfall beyond that. Here the easy hike ends and the very difficult hike begins.

There are two very difficult routes around these waterfalls. You might want to set a throw bag or belay on this section for safety. The first route, on creek left, is up a 40 foot high crack-chimney just 100 feet or so before the first narrows waterfall. From the top of this chimney, there is a ledge that leads along and up a bit 1/8 mile back to the creek bed. The other route is to climb up to the top of the first narrows waterfall. At the top of this waterfall, you'll need to climb a 5 foot high ledge with very small handholds on creek left. Once above this ledge, you will be able to climb up to the ledge coming from the lower route, and proceed up and along 1/8 mile back into the creek bed. Once past this very difficult up-climb, you are hiking in the Hualapai Nation and a day-use permit is required. From here, the canyon floor becomes a series of pools and patios. If a gravel flood has recently swept through, the pools will be full of gravel, but if it's a hot summer day and the pools are free of gravel, it's your lucky day for a swim. In winter, you can walk around all these pools without getting wet.

Beyond these pools, you can expect about 1 1/2 miles of boulder hopping. Then a small tributary comes in from the east. From here, you have a very limited view of the Flatirons, a formation of tilted fins in the Coconino skyline about 1 1/2 miles away to the east. There is a fine permanent spring in the wash another 1/2 mile up the canyon. It's another 2-mile walk to the top of the Redwall. You still can't get a view of where the heck you are. There is a nice shelter camp on creek left just before the wash tops through the Redwall. From here, National Canyon continues on up through the Supai into a sun-drenched, north-south trending, wide canyon. This is really fine country, and you may see a wild horse or two up here. It's a long way back to camp.

145

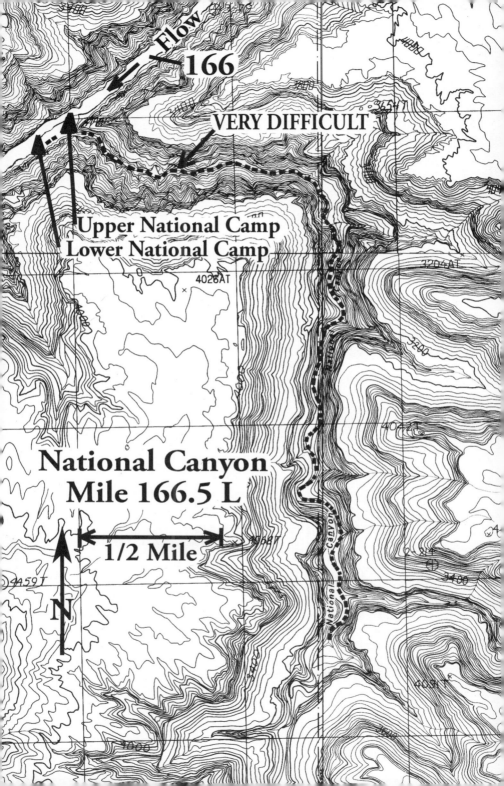

Flow
166
VERY DIFFICULT
Upper National Camp
Lower National Camp

National Canyon
Mile 166.5 L

1/2 Mile

N

64. Fern Glen Canyon

There is a great camp on river right just below the rapid at the mouth of Fern Glen Canyon (Mile 168.0 R), so big that two trips could share the beach if they camped on either end. There is a nice, short, easy hike of 1/2 mile or so here into some delicious shade in the heat of summer.

From camp, hike into the mouth and up the drainage of Fern Glen Canyon. The canyon quickly turns west, hiding from the sun. There is a permanent seep in this section of the drainage. You need to climb past a small waterfall on creek left to hike up to the fine amphitheater with a small waterfall at its back. The helevac-minded might want to try their luck climbing the more-than-very-difficult travertine waterfall. They will find, if they make it to the top of the falls, a large plunge pool, and an even harder climb out the creek-left side of the pool. Most folk enjoy the shade at the foot of the waterfalls.

Of note is the Fern Glen Arch, also called Alamo Arch, just above Fern Glen in the Redwall on the north side of the river. The best place to see the arch is from the middle of the Fern Glen Rapid, when most folk should be looking to make sure they go right or left of that pourover in the middle of the river. You can also get a good view of the arch if you pull to shore on river left at the top of the rapid and follow the trail over to the base of the cliffs on river left. Look across the river and north up into the Redwall. The arch is in a Redwall buttress coming toward you, so though you can appreciate that there is an arch here, you really don't have too good a view of it. This arch is supposed to be the biggest Redwall arch in the Canyon.

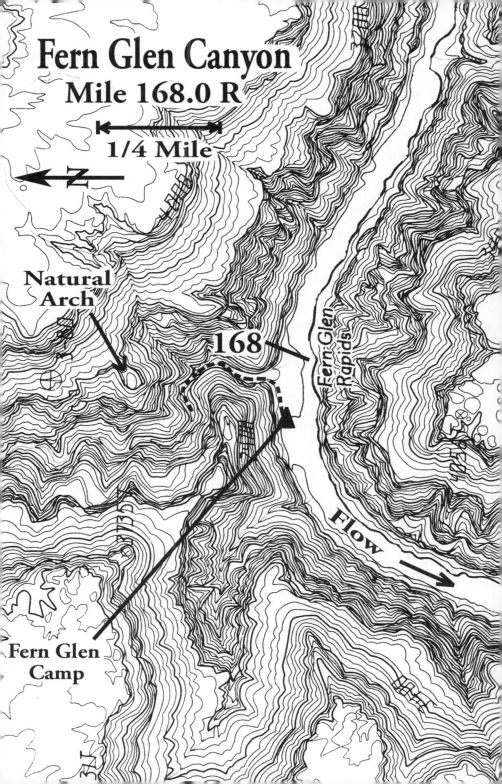

Fern Glen Canyon
Mile 168.0 R

1/4 Mile

N

Natural
Arch

168

Fern Glen Rapids

Flow

Fern Glen
Camp

65. Stairway Canyon

Forget that willow-choked camp at Mohawk (hike #66) and camp here! This fine camp, with some winter sun and lots of summer sun, is on a point (Mile 171.0 R) just above the mouth of the Stairway Canyon wash, and the pull-in is right at the tip of the point. There are a couple of great hikes you can do here.

The really expert climbers in your group might want to try their luck at climbing the very difficult and dangerous Stairway Tower. To attempt this climb, walk up the Stairway Canyon wash around the rock tower on creek right. It's only a few hundred yards. Hike west and back a little south up to the saddle between the tower and the main limestone cliffs. Hike back about halfway around the south side of the tower and look for a chimney up. Work your way up this chimney to the ridge top just west of the tower itself. Cross the ridge to the north side and look for another chimney up to the base of the last blocks. You will notice that the blocks that make up the tower are stacked a little offset, so that the last block teeters precariously on top of the one below it. If you decide to actually climb the last block, from the top you will have a really great view straight down the other side to the bottom of the Stairway wash that you are now overhanging in free space. With luck, you will want to return the way you came.

For a much smarter hike, there is a great easy walk up the Stairway drainage. There is a small spring about 1/2 mile from camp. It gets fairly brushy in here, and there is one small pourover with a pool of water at its base that is easy to slip into if you are not careful. There is a large boulder you have to walk under in the narrows another 1/2 mile up, and from here the going gets difficult as you will need to climb 80 feet or so up out of the drainage on creek right to bypass a large waterfall.

Just after this waterfall there is a fork in the drainage. From here, there is a very difficult hike out through the Redwall. You will need to hike up the ridge between these two drainages to the base of the Redwall, then skirt into the west side of the east drainage. Continue along the base of the cliff until you come to a section that has a chute going up it. It is up this chute that you must go to get through the Redwall. At the top of this chute there is a vertical cliff, but over to your right is a small crack system going up through the cliff. It is near-vertical with only a small crack for protection, but that's the route. Once you pass this point, you are at the top of the Redwall.

Stairway Canyon
Mile 171.0 R

N

1/2 Mile

VERY
DIFFICULT

Stairway Canyon

Flow

Stairway
Tower
VERY
DIFFICULT

Gateway
Rapids

171

Stairway Canyon
Camp

Mohawk Camp

65. Stairway Canyon contd.

But wait, if this is not enough for you, you can hike along the top of the Redwall on the west side of Stairway Canyon back out to the river. You have only one large bay to skirt, and along the way there is a nice Redwall arch you can hike out on top of.

The Stairway Arch is much smaller than the Fern Glen Arch. Continue on south to the point at which the Redwall bends to the west and on downriver. There is a great view from here straight down into camp, the mouth of Mohawk Canyon and Gateway Rapid. The view up and downriver is also stunning. Unfortunately, you are about 3 miles from camp and a good thousand feet over it. Sorry, but the return is via your up-climb. This is a great late fall, winter or early spring hike. Don't even think about climbing up here in the summer. As usual, be mindful of the small native vegetation, which has only you to protect it by not treading on it. The camp here, like all the Canyon's camps, needs us to do our part in cleaning up any trash we find, not just ours but anyone else's.

66. Mohawk Canyon

Tucked away just above Lava Falls is a gem of a canyon called Mohawk. At River Mile 171.5 L, Mohawk is usually missed because it's hot and the only thing most folk are thinking about is that rapid 8 miles downstream called Lava Falls. But if the weather is not too hot and you're up for something off the beaten path, try this on for size.

The pull-in for this camp is at the foot of Gateway Rapid on river left. There is a large eddy here and the camp is at the uppermost end of the eddy. There is not a lot of shade here in mid-summer, but there is some winter sun.

Once you have left the boats, hike around to the creekbed and walk up-drainage. You are entering Hualapai Nation land once you hike away from the river and will need a day-use permit to proceed. After 1/2 mile or so the creekbed cuts through some Muav narrows, and in the fall, winter and spring, there is running water and some fine small waterfalls here. A mile or more from the river, there is a small waterfall that is easiest to climb around on creek left (that's the west side of the creekbed). There is no water above the top of the falls if you stay in the main drainage. After hiking up drainage another mile, look for a large living-room size boulder in the creekbed. This is your sign to climb up 150 feet to the base of the cliffs on creek left again. Follow this bench for about 1/3 mile back into the creek bottom. This gets you around two chockstone pourovers. From here, you can walk right on up the creekbed through the Redwall. Near the top of the Redwall you may be lucky and see a wild burro or two.

There are down-sides to this hike, even in the best of weather. This hike takes you right into the Las Vegas to the South Rim scenic air tour flight zones. This is a busy flight path, so expect a lot of low-flying planes flying overhead.

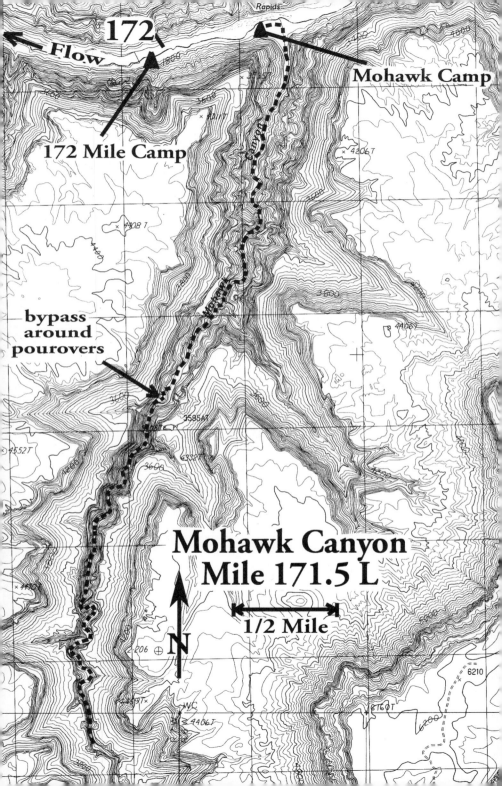

172

← **Flow**

172 Mile Camp

Rapids

Mohawk Camp

**bypass
around
pourovers**

**Mohawk Canyon
Mile 171.5 L**

1/2 Mile

N

67. Cove Canyon

A short walk from a nice camp makes Cove Canyon an enjoyable camp. There are actually two camps here at Mile 174.3 R. The upper camp is at the top of the Cove Canyon debris fan, while the lower camp is at the point at the very top of the Cove Canyon riffle.

From camp, there is a path leading up creek-left into the canyon bottom. Stay on this path to protect the native vegetation. In 1/4 mile from the river you will come to a natural dam made of rock-fall blocking the drainage. You will need to pick your way through this rock jumble to proceed. There's a flat gravel bottom above this natural dam with a large amount of tamarisk. You can proceed another 1/4 mile or less to a stopper waterfall. Cove Canyon is a mystery to me above this point. Some other time. It's a toaster in this south- facing canyon in the summer time, though early morning or late afternoon can be pleasant enough.

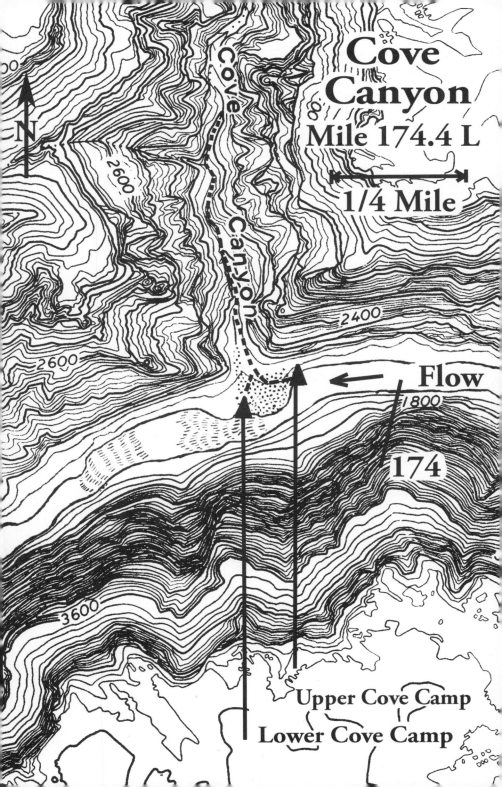

Cove Canyon

Cove Canyon

Mile 174.4 L

1/4 Mile

N

2600

2600

2400

Flow

1800

174

3600

Upper Cove Camp

Lower Cove Camp

68. Prospect Canyon

Lava Falls is one of the biggest rapids you will run on your trip. The falls are the result of many tons worth of debris washing into the river from the Prospect Canyon drainage to the south. This drainage covers an area of over 100 square miles, and the last mile of the wash drops over 3000 feet. This combination of a quick drop in elevation and a big drainage area that lies behind it sets the stage for the "fire hose turned loose in a gravel pit" analogy, meaning that if any rapid has the potential to change (read get worse), this is it. There is some difficult hiking to be done on this side of the river from a good little camp on river left just above Lava, at Mile 179.0 L. It can take the better part of a day to explore Prospect, so planning for a layover here is a good idea. Given that you will be camping just above Lava, and that summer temperatures are in the 100s, make sure this is a group decision.

You are entering Hualapai Nation land once you hike away from the river and will need a day-use permit to proceed. The best way to hike up the drainage is to walk downstream from camp along the Colorado to the mouth of the wash, then turn south and walk up the wash. There will be a few pourovers to work around, but this will be much easier than heading overland straight out of camp to intercept the wash farther up in the drainage. If you take the overland route, be forewarned. There is a very steep band of gravel cliffs you will have to find a way through to get into the drainage if you go this way. To make things worse, you will find a copious amount of catclaw acacia, which is not the brush of choice to have to make your way through on a very steep slope.

Continue on up the steep drainage. After a mile, you will find that the wash comes over a 200-foot-plus-high pourover on the west side of the drainage. You will also see that you can keep on hiking south up a steep cinder pile. You will have to skirt a few basalt flows, but at last you will reach the top of the cinders and crest a small ridge of river gravels. At the top of this gravel ridge, you will suddenly have a view of the huge Prospect Canyon drainage stretching away to the south. Vulcan's Throne will be dominating the northern skyline, just 2 1/2 miles straight across the river. From this vantage point, you will be able to see where all the gravels are coming from that create Lava Falls, and appreciate that Lava Falls will be with us in its majestic way for a long time to come.

Though this hike is only 1 1/2 miles as the crow flies, it's an impressive elevation gain through loose cinder and sand up a tight canyon. If it's raining, you may be peppered by falling debris from the canyon sides, and if it's a hot day, don't even think about hiking up this drainage.

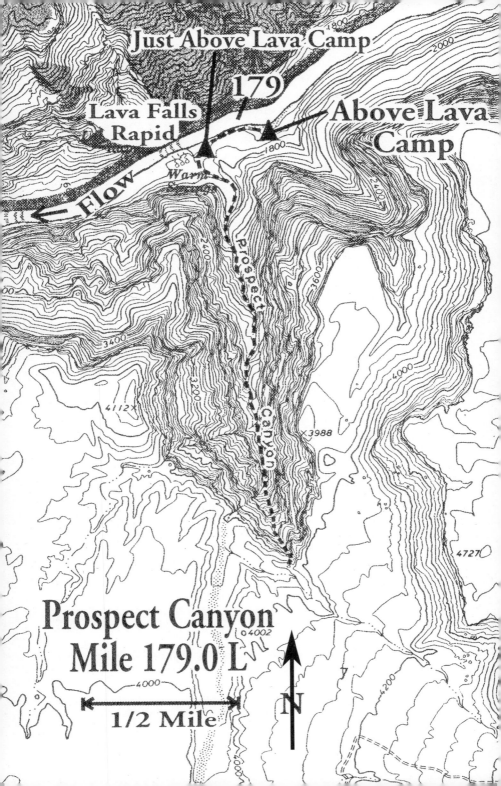

Just Above Lava Camp

179

Above Lava Camp

Lava Falls
Rapid

Flow

Warn

Prospect

Canyon

×3988

4112×

3400

3200

2400

1800

1800

2000

2400

3600

4000

4727

4002

4000

4200

Prospect Canyon
Mile 179.0 L

1/2 Mile

N

69. Vulcan's Throne

Lava day can also be a great day for a very enjoyable but difficult hike, especially on a cool fall, cool winter or cool spring day. Note the emphasis on COOL. Vulcan's Throne is a 1000-foot-high circular cinder cone sitting on top of the Esplanade. It's only a mile from Lava Falls, but its summit is 3500 feet above the river. The hike up the Toroweap Route (also known as the Lava Falls Trail) is steep, but the views from the top are fantastic. It should be understood that this hike will be in the "stupid" stinking hot hikes category if undertaken in hot weather. Be forewarned, there is NO shade on this hike.

The route starts at River Mile 179.0 right, at the bend in the river where the spray from Lava Falls just comes into view. There's a good camp on river left here, by the way (see hike #68). With a little planning, you can layover at the camp on the left and row across the river to spend the day hiking on river right. The route winds its way up sharply through numerous basalt flows and then goes up a steep cinder slope. The true meaning of "multiple trailing" really shows here, as you can hike up one path and on your return journey come down a completely different one. Try as much as you can to stay on the main trail here. This section is very very steep. The route finally traverses around to a small drainage, and (puff puff) levels off somewhat. Once in the drainage, a short walk takes you to where the trail meets the end of the Toroweap Lake road. There is a sign-in register at this point. The comments section makes for fun reading. At this point you have just hiked up through the Redwall and into the Supai. Don't look for any, as everything is covered by cinders and the occasional bit of basalt.

From the register at the end of the road, proceed easterly, or back upriver, climbing up the cinder slope of Vulcan's Throne. The top is a C-shaped ridge, with the highest point on the east side. Wouldn't you know it, you've just come up the west side and now have to hike around the top to the far side to reach the summit. But do it! The views are fantastic. To the south is Prospect Canyon, with a great view of that drainage's plunge down to the raging torrent of Lava Falls. To the east and south a bit is Mollies Nipple, about 20 miles away and on the other side of Parashant Wash. To the north is Lake Toroweap, the dry pan beyond which stretches the Toroweap Valley. Toroweap Point defines the end of the cliffs coming toward you on the eastern border of Toroweap Valley. Got that? Hey, don't go to sleep here, because to the east by 20 miles you can see Mount Sinyella, on the other side of Havasu Canyon, no less.

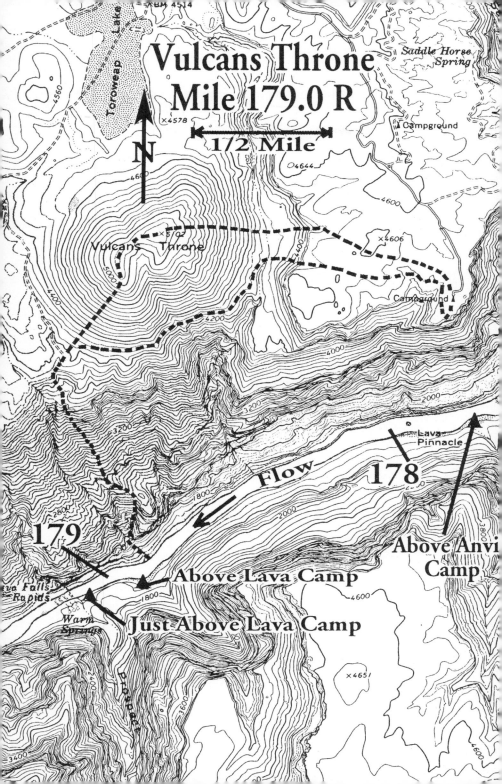

Vulcans Throne
Mile 179.0 R

N

|← 1/2 Mile →|

Toroweap Lake

×BM 4514

Saddle Horse Spring

×4578

Campground

○4644

4600

Vulcans Throne

×502

×4606

×4600

Campground

4200

4000

Lava Pinnacle

Flow

178

2000

179

Above Anvil Camp

Lava Falls Rapids

Above Lava Camp

Warm Springs

Just Above Lava Camp

1800

4600

×4651

4600

69. Vulcan's Throne contd.

You can go right back to the boats the way you came, but the industrious hiker may want to see the Toroweap overlook, where so many photos of the Canyon are taken, which is only another mile away. To get to the overlook, proceed down the east side of Vulcan's Throne, then go across a small valley and up the other side, continuing east. The basalt ends, replaced by the sandstone of the Esplanade. You will intercept a small road going to the overlook. Turn right (south) and walk the short distance to the end of the road. There are no guardrails here, and the drop is impressive. There are good views of Lava Falls from here, but you will get an eyeful of Lava soon enough. Retrace your path into the small valley at the base of Vulcan's, and contour around the cinder cone to the south. It's tough going, side stepping on a steep slope trying to keep those pesky cinders out of your shoes. There is a small game trail going your way, so keep an eye out for it, as the journey is much easier on this path. You should end up on the gentle slope near the end of the Toroweap Lake road and the start of the Toroweap Trail, intercepting the route you took earlier in the day.

This is one of those hikes you just don't want to take in the heat of summer. Period. You'll come back to camp totally toasted to find those folks with enough sense not to follow you even hotter and worse off than you. As always, stay hydrated and eat salty snack foods.

70. Hell's Hollow

Hell's Hollow is a wonderful spot to do an easy or a very difficult hike. Yes, it is hot here in the summer, and these are not mid-summer hikes. Still, if it's cool enough, there's some really great hiking from a nice camp at Mile 182.8 L. There's a basalt boulder in the middle of the river less than 1/4 mile above this camp. Once you see that boulder, think Hell's Hollow. The name here is actually a little misleading. Hell's Hollow is a side canyon entering the river at Mile 182.6 L. The 3 1/2 mile hike described here is in the fault-controlled drainage just downstream from the Hell's Hollow drainage.

From camp, hike downstream to the southwest and cross the drainage bottom, then turn south and hike up the ridge just west of the drainage bottom. In 1/4 mile you will crest a small saddle. This is the easy hike, though you could proceed along the game trail you will find here and contour into the drainage below to check that out. The folks doing the very difficult hike will come back this way. The very difficult hike starts here. From this saddle, contour west less than 1/8 mile around to a chute going up into the Redwall. Take this chute back up to the ridge top. Proceed around to the south side of the ridge and continue working your way west. In less than 1/4 mile you will come to a 10-foot drop. This is the very difficult part. You will find a small ledge to let your self down onto, from which you can then work your way to the base of this drop. From here, proceed up and west again, to the top of the Redwall, then head west and north to skirt the unnamed Supai butte due west of you. Contour around the butte into the drainage to the west of the butte, then climb up through broken Supai to the butte top. From here the view is amazing. The Dome by Tuckup is 20 miles to your east, with Vulcan's Throne just across the river. To get a view to the west, head southwest up onto the Esplanade, then overland a little over 1/2 mile to the northwest out onto the Esplanade fin shown on the map. Whitmore Wash is now in clear view to the west. From here, hike 1 1/4 miles due south over the rolling Esplanade, following watercourses and exposed sandstone to avoid the crust soils, back to the head of the fault-controlled drainage you hiked the north side of already. Proceed south past the drainage top about 200 yards to broken Supai ledges, which you can work down 150 feet or so. Then traverse back into the drainage proper above a 50-foot cliff. (It may be better to go 1/4 mile to the east-southeast and drop into the drainage there, though I have not done this.) Once you get into the drainage, head down it. You will have to down-climb two short chimneys. Once past these, the drainage will be an easy walk for 1 1/2 miles back to the point below the small saddle you were at earlier in the day. Hike up to the saddle and on back to camp. Please note that this is a very difficult and challenging hike. Be sure to take ample food and water.

186.0 Left Camp ▲ 186

185.5 Right Camp ▲

185.3 Right Camp ▲ 185

184.5 Left Camp

184

Flow

VERY DIFFICULT

183

Below Chevron Camp

Lower Chevron Camp

Hells Hollow Mile 182.8 L

1/2 Mile

Below Old Helipad Camp

182.8 Left Camp

Upper Chevron Camp

182

71. Whitmore Trail

Whitmore Trail is another place with a lot to do: there is a short easy hike to a small archaeological site with pictographs, or a little longer easy hike to the nearby rim. Either one is an enjoyable stroll. The pull-in for these hikes is at the sandy beach at 187.75 R. The pull-in can be a little tricky as there is an eddy just above this point with current going back upstream, while below here a strong current goes on downriver. You may have to share airspace with a low-flying helicopter exchanging commercial river trip passengers just upstream.

From the pull-in, you will see a small path leading away from the river into a large thicket of arrowweed. The path leads straight about 100 yards to a small archaeological site that dates back over 2000 years. A stabilizing wall built by the Park Service protects the dwelling from erosion. Just south a few yards along the cliff from this dwelling are some nice pictographs above you. As with all rock art, don't touch it. The oils on your hand can ruin this priceless art.

From here, you might want to hike the mile-long trail to the rim on the Whitmore Wash Trail. To get to the trail, walk upriver from the dwelling until you reach the well-used trail. It's an easy walk to the rim. You may spot pieces of black plastic pipe going down through the cliffs; it was used as a refueling line by early river runners. At the rim, you will find an old line shack used by the local ranchers, some of whom have signed their names on the walls inside, like the famous Bundies and Heatons. The return walk is the reverse of your up-climb.

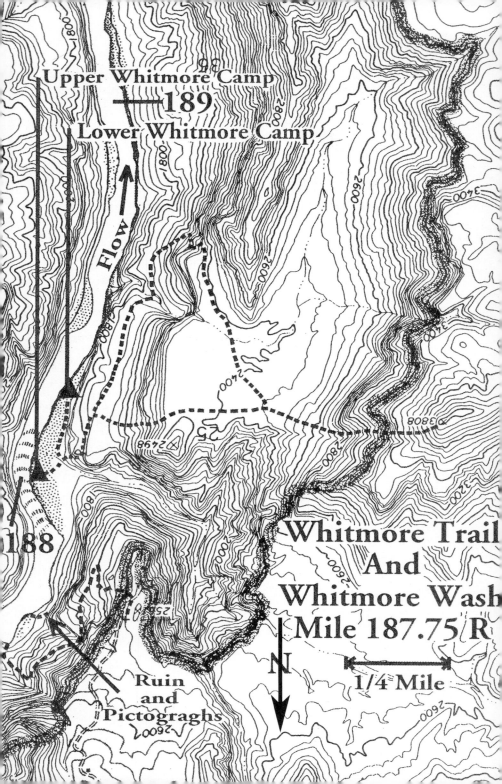

Upper Whitmore Camp
189
Lower Whitmore Camp

Flow

188

Whitmore Trail
And
Whitmore Wash
Mile 187.75 R

N

1/4 Mile

Ruin
and
Pictograghs

72. Whitmore Wash

There are two camps at Whitmore Wash, but clearly the upper camp, just above Whitmore Rapid, at Mile 188.0 R, is the camp of choice. The lower camp, at the foot of the rapid, is less sheltered from the wind. From either camp, there is some easy exploring to do. Folks can hike back upriver to hike the Whitmore Trail (hike #71), or can hike the 1 1/2 miles to the unnamed butte just to the west of this camp. The butte is the one visible on the straight stretch of river just upstream. Now is as good a time as any to remind everyone about camp stewardship. Leave your camp cleaner than when you arrived. This hike is for a cool day or a mild cloudy day. Hiking in black basalt in full sun on a summer day is not recommended.

To hike to the butte, you will want to hike up the trail leading up the ridge just behind camp and on the south side of Whitmore Wash. You will find a small corral hidden behind a large basalt boulder. From here proceed south 1/8 mile, then west through a low line of cliffs to reach a flat bench. Proceed back 1/8 mile northwest, then go up the small drainage back to the southwest. In another 1/8 mile you will reach another flat intermediate bench. From here, proceed due west 3/4 mile up through the broken Supai. You should not have to do any difficult hiking here if you pick and choose your way through the Supai. You will cross a small trail here going north and south. Keep this trail in mind for the return hike. But for now, continue climbing right up to the summit of the butte, at an elevation of 3808 feet. There is a nice view from this butte top. You are a couple of thousand feet above the river at this point. Vulcan's Throne (at least the south side of it) is visible to the northeast. The line shack at the top of Whitmore Trail is also to the northeast. Whitmore Point is to the northwest, and Dr. Tommy Mountain is to the south.

The return is as you have come. Alternatively, there's another stock trail leading down to the river. To take this route, hike back down to the intermediate plain below, where you noted the north-south running trail. Proceed southeast across this plain and cross the drainage coming in from the south. You will be on top of a basalt cliff. Follow this cliff south and look for the top of the trail heading down just at the tip of the basalt cliff. This trail has a lot of stone work at its top, then winds down to the lower bench. You will want to be sure not to miss the trail forking. One fork goes south, but you want to take the trail going back to the north. Proceed back north, passing a basalt pourover from the drainage you crossed above on the intermediate bench. Continue north on this level 1/2 mile back to the corral you were at this morning, and retrace your steps to camp. Sstay on the trail as much as possible to avoid stepping on the fragile desert crusts.

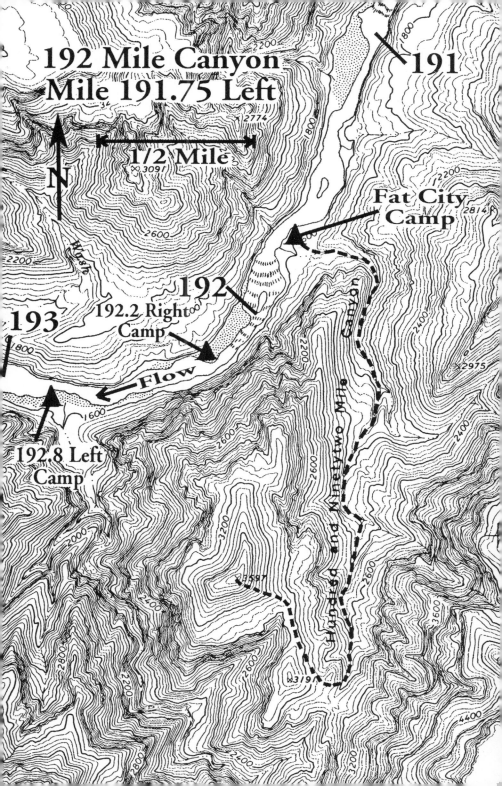

192 Mile Canyon
Mile 191.75 Left

N

1/2 Mile

191

Fat City Camp

192

192.2 Right Camp

193

Flow

192.8 Left Camp

Hundred and Ninetytwo Mile Canyon

73. 192 Mile Canyon

Fat City is a great camp, with fine winter sun and morning summer shade. Plus, there is a nice easy hike out behind camp. It's easy to be in the middle of the river and see the camp too late to make the pull-in. At water stages of 20 thousand cfs and less, keep an eye out for a small cobble bar in the middle of the river (191.5) and once past this bar move over to river left. The pull-in (Mile 191.75 L) is on a sand bank coming down to the water's edge. There is often enough driftwood around for a good warm winter fire.

There is a great hike from here along the Hurricane Fault just behind camp. You are entering Hualapai Nation land once you hike away from the river and will need a day-use permit to proceed. Hike up the drainage just behind camp to the east. This drainage bends south into the fault, and in 1/2 mile or more forks. Take the smaller south fork, hiking up the west side of the drainage around the pourover you quickly encounter. From here, it's a gradual climb up the drainage another 3/4 mile to a saddle at the head of the drainage. Hike north-west another 1/2 mile past one small butte to the top of the larger one behind it. There is a little scrambling through 10-foot-high cliff bands to gain the top of this unnamed Supai butte.

There is a great view from here south into the rolling hills of the 193 Mile drainage (hike # 74), certainly not the landscape you expect to see in Grand Canyon. To the west is the Parashant and Andrus Canyon's drainage with Mollies Nipple on the skyline, while to the north is Whitmore Canyon and the Toroweap Volcanic Field. To your east is an impressive cliff of Redwall Limestone towering over you, as you stand on your Supai perch. This offset of strata is the result of the Hurricane Fault between you and the cliffs just to the east. This is a short, less-than-half-day walk. There is no shade here in the summer.

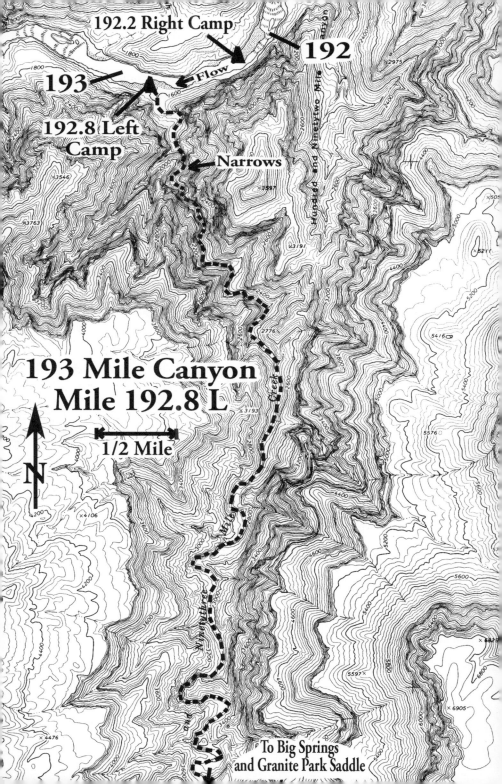

192.2 Right Camp

192

193

192.8 Left Camp

Flow

Narrows

Hundred and Ninetytwo Mile Canyon

193 Mile Canyon
Mile 192.8 L

1/2 Mile

N

193 Mile Creek

Ninetythree Mile

To Big Springs
and Granite Park Saddle

74. 193 Mile Canyon

One Hundred Ninety-Three Mile Canyon offers something for everyone, from an easy hour-long hike into cool narrows on a hot summer day to a difficult all-day hike over to the northern edge of the Granite Park drainage. If you want to do a winter layover and spend all day hiking far, there is a nice camp with a lot of firewood and sun at the foot of the 193 Mile Canyon riffle (Mile 192.75 L). The pull-in is at the top of the eddy just below the riffle on river left. In the summer, you sure won't want to camp in this shadeless hot spot. You could camp at the 192 Mile camp (Mile 191.75 L), come down here to hike for the day, then head to 194 Mile (Mile 194.0 L) for camp. You are entering Hualapai Nation land once you hike away from the river and will need a day-use permit to proceed.

The 193 Mile drainage follows the Hurricane Fault, creating a twisting canyon that goes in and out of the Redwall, depending on which side of the fault you are on. For a short hike into some rather impressive narrows, head south up the 193 Mile wash from the pull-in. In less than 1/2 mile, the wash narrows in and forms some impressive limestone narrows. There is deep shade here in a spot where you can touch both walls of this tight narrows with outstretched hands. If it's a cool day and you have the time, you can head right on up the main drainage. About 1/2 mile from the river, a fault drainage will enter from the southwest. You want to stay in the main drainage, which heads off to the south at this junction. About a mile from the river, the 193 Mile drainage crosses the Hurricane Fault, re-crosses it, and crosses it again. The interplay between rock types is impressive here.

Stay in the main drainage for another 5 miles as it heads south, with tributaries joining it from the west and east. About 6 miles from the river, the tributary forks, with the Big Springs arm coming in from the east. There are some unclimbable Redwall narrows if you head up the Big Springs arm, so keep going south another 1 1/2 miles to the saddle between the 193 and Granite Park drainages. It's a little brushy near the top of the saddle. From here, if you have the energy, hike 1/4 mile east to the top of the broken Supai cliffs making up the eastern side of the saddle. This area has been called the heart of the west end of Grand Canyon, and the view is fantastic. The Toroweap volcanic fields and Hell's Hollow are 20 miles to the north, and yes, that is Diamond Peak roughly 16 miles to the south-southwest. You are a very long way from camp here, and in the summer, you do not want to attempt this hike. There is no water available on this hike, so bring enough fluids and food to last the day.

195

← Flow

194 Mile Camp →

Hualapai Acres Camp

194 Mile Canyon
Mile 194.5 L

N

1/2 Mile

75. 194 Mile Canyon

There is a great big sandy camp (Mile 194.1 L) 1/2 mile above 194 Mile Canyon, and this camp is a lot better than the one (Mile 194.5 L) at the mouth of 194 Mile Canyon. The upper camp has early shade and late sun in the summer. If you are going to attempt the difficult hike up 194 to the Esplanade, you should layover at the upper camp. Better you struggle through a little extra brush to get down to the drainage and those who stay behind enjoy a great camp, than you get easy access to 194, and those who stay behind spend the day at a not-so-great camp.

You are entering Hualapai Nation land once you hike away from the river and will need a day-use permit to proceed. To hike into 194 from the upper camp, hike up the upstream side of the basalt flow behind camp, over the top of this flow and back downstream at this level the 1/2 mile down to 194 Mile Canyon. Head on up the drainage. In a mile there is a fork, with a drainage coming in from the south. Stay in the main drainage, going southwest. In another mile, hike out of the drainage on creek left up through the broken Supai to the Esplanade. Climbing the small rise 1/4 mile to the north will give you a great view of the Hell's Hollow Volcanic Fields 20 miles to the north, Mollies Nipple to the west, and the northern corner of Dr. Tommy Mountain to the south. You will have to share the air space with the many tour flights out of Las Vegas going to the Tusayan Airport and back to Vegas. The return is as you came. Enjoy.

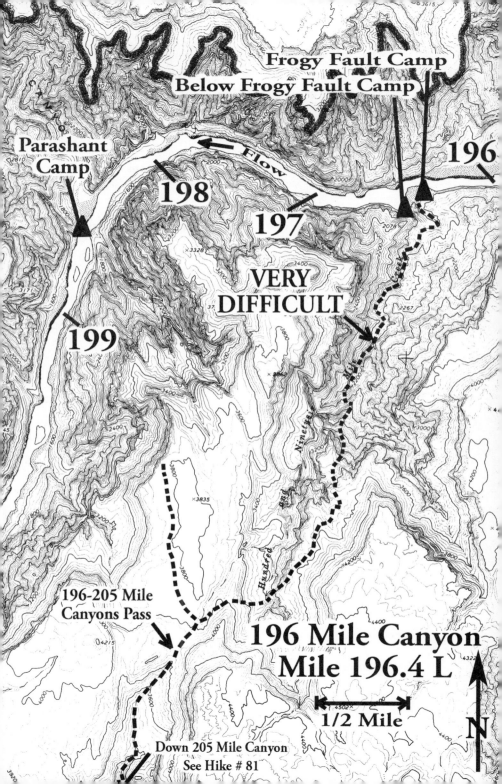

Frogy Fault Camp

Below Frogy Fault Camp

Parashant
Camp

Flow

196

198

197

VERY
DIFFICULT

199

196-205 Mile
Canyons Pass

196 Mile Canyon
Mile 196.4 L

1/2 Mile

N

Down 205 Mile Canyon
See Hike # 81

76. 196 Mile Canyon

The Froggy Fault camp at Mile 196.4 L is a rough camp on a debris fan prone to flooding in monsoon season. So why would anyone want to camp here, particularly given that there's a very difficult pourover blocking access to the upper reaches of this drainage 3/4 mile from the river? Because, well, you can hike from here to 205 Mile, that's why. Now look, this is not only a very difficult hike, but includes the following danger. The boats have to go downriver 9 miles, while the hikers will go 7 miles overland, including having to deal with the pourover in 196 Mile Canyon and the Redwall in 205. This hike gets a very difficult logistical rating as well.

First of all, if you are going to do this up-and-over hike, you can't miss the pull-in. It's just before the river turns sharply to the left at Mile 196.4. Don't attempt this hike in the heat. If the hikers cannot make it past the pourover up 196, they will have to hike downriver 9 miles. Only trouble is, 1/8 mile below 196 Mile, there are cliffs into the river, so you would have to hike up and around them, then hike through miles and miles of riverside vegetation to catch up with your group. The folks with the boats will have to row on down to 205 Mile Rapid. They should hang at the top of the rapid (Mile 205.4 L), where there is no camp, and give 205 Mile Rapid a good scout, then pull into the small beach on river left at the foot of the rapid at Mile 205.5 L. Here they will have to wait for the hikers. If they miss the pull-in, then the hikers will have to hike on downriver another mile, hiking up and over more cliffs into the river. Again, this is a very difficult logistical hike and a very difficult hike. You are entering Hualapai Nation land once you hike away from the river and will need a day-use permit to proceed.

Here's the hike. From the 196.4 Mile camp, head up the 196 Mile drainage. In 3/4 mile the drainage forks. The southeast fork is an unclimable pourover here. The south fork has a deep pool of water to swim through, or a very difficult ridge to climb up between the two forks to get around the pool. The ridge leads 50 feet up to the base of a 60-foot-high cliff. Hike southwest along the base of this cliff back into the south drainage. Hike up the drainage another 1/4 mile or so. You will see a huge Redwall pourover, and a chute going up through the Redwall just to the east of this pourover. Up that chute you go. It would appear to be possible to traverse out of this chute at the top of the pourover back into the drainage on the low side of the Froggy Fault. We did not try this, given that the boats were gone. Continue up the chute all the way to the Redwall top on the high side of the Froggy Fault. Once you top out of the Redwall, proceed southeast another 1/8 mile across a small fault and up the hillside again to the

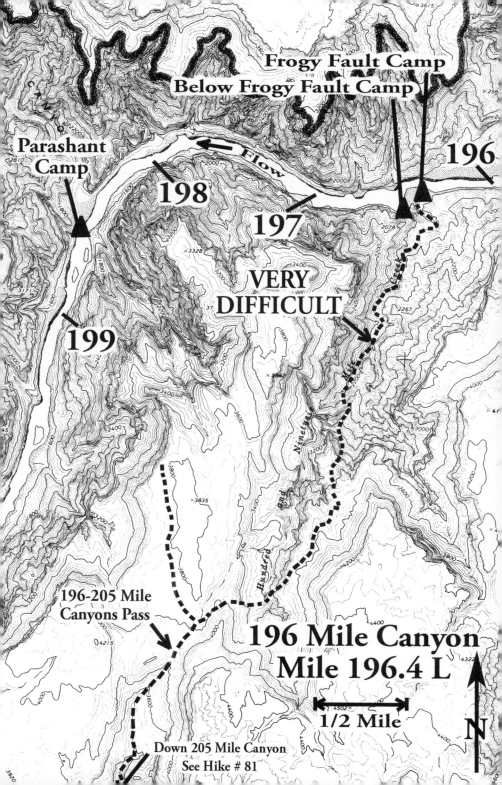

Frogy Fault Camp

Below Frogy Fault Camp

Flow

196

Parashant
Camp

198

197

VERY
DIFFICULT

199

196-205 Mile
Canyons Pass

196 Mile Canyon
Mile 196.4 L

1/2 Mile

N

Down 205 Mile Canyon
See Hike # 81

76. 196 Mile Canyon contd.

top of the Redwall. There's a good view of Mollies Nipple from here, but more on that later.

Nothing for it now but to head south-southwest along the Redwall 3/4 of a mile. Notice how the drainage is getting closer to you as you proceed in this direction. There is an easy break down through the Redwall where the south fork turns slightly southeast. Cross the drainage, and head 1/2 mile southwest to the 196-205 Mile saddle. If you have made it to here in good shape, then maybe a small side journey is called for. If you hike due north for a mile on the top of the Esplanade here, you can come to the rim's edge 3 miles east and across the canyon from Mollies Nipple. The view down to 202 and Parashant is very nice. This is a fine place for lunch.

Still, the boats, friends and camp are a long way off. Hike back to the 196-205 Mile saddle, and begin the walk down 205. In 1999, 205 flashed heavily. In the spring of 2000, we found an adult alligator juniper tree smashed to toothpicks in the drainage floor. This is a powerful warning to stay out of drainages in monsoon season. About 1 1/2 miles from the saddle, you will hike out of the Supai and into some wonderful limestone narrows. As this drainage is fault-dominated, you will hike into and out of the Redwall and Supai depending on which side of the fault the drainage is on. If it has recently rained, you will have to wade or swim through two water pockets here. In another mile, you come to a second set of Redwall narrows. At this point, you need to find a way down through the Redwall. Hike south-southwest along the Redwall top for 1/4 mile. You will find a very difficult 60-foot cliff face with adequate hand and foot holds to get down here. On the map, it appears as though there may be an easier route another 1/8 mile along. Also, if you hike 3/4 mile in this south-southeast direction, you will come to a fault section that has decimated the integrity of the Redwall, allowing a slope hike back to the 205 Mile drainage.

However you get there, do it carefully and safely. Once you gain the drainage below the Redwall, you are still 2 1/2 miles from the river. Continue down the drainage bottom until you intersect the route as in hike # 81. Hike right down the drainage to the river and 205 Mile Rapid. Think long and hard about this one—it is long and hard.

77. Parashant Canyon and the Book of Worms

Parashant Canyon offers a lot of hiking opportunities from a great camp. The camp is at the foot of the riffle made by the Parashant drainage entering on river right (Mile 198.5 R). This large camp offers early afternoon shade and late morning sun in an otherwise hot west end of Grand Canyon. The pull-in is hidden, so stay close to the right shoreline as you approach the Parashant riffle and be ready to make the cut right as soon as you see a large eddy and obvious camp. This is a highly used summer camp because of the shade and easy hiking, so help out and make sure this camp is like all the others you have stayed at, really clean when you leave.

Those who want to stay close to camp might enjoy looking at the agave roasting pit on the upstream side of the Parashant wash from camp, and then calling it good enough. Hike into the wash behind camp, and then go a couple of hundred yards up the drainage. You will pass old high water sediments on the creek-left side of the wash. As these sediments thin, look for a trail leading away from the wash onto a flat terrace. Once there, look for a 25 foot-diameter, slightly raised mound. This roasting pit is an oven of sorts, and was used by Ancestral Puebloan folk to bake the tuberous root of the agave plant. Think baked potatoes and you get the rough idea. You can recognize the spot by its plentiful supply of small cracked rock and charcoal from the fire used to heat the rock covering the agave. This is an archaeological site, and like all other sites in the Canyon, needs us to protect it. Don't walk on the site, and stay on the trail here so that we can protect the desert soil crusts as well.

You may want to stretch your legs and hike all day up the 7 easy miles of gravel wash to the Copper Mountain Mine and Parashant narrows. And then, some of you might want to just hike 1/8 mile up the wash bottom from camp, and look at the Book of Worms. This is a garage sized-block of Bright Angel Shale that has fallen on its side, landing just outside the wash bottom on creek left only a few hundred yards upstream of the trail leading to the agave pit. The many worm burrows in the soft green shale are a sprightly 550 million years old. The Book is lying on its spine. It's a squat book, and massive too. Happy reading.

Parashant Canyon
and the
Book of Worms
Mile 198.5 R

N

1/2 Mile

Roasting Pit

Book of Worms

Flow

Parashant
Camp

78. Parashant Canyon to Mollies Nipple

The Parashant Canyon camp (see pull-in information at hike # 77) offers a very challenging and very difficult hike to Mollies Nipple. This very difficult hike requires some very good route-finding skills. The nutters in your group might want to try this very difficult hike out to the Esplanade and Mollies Nipple, as it's only 2 1/2 miles and all day away. Note the use of the words "very difficult" four times. Hmm…

To climb Mollies Nipple, you will need to find your way out through the broken limestone cliffs just behind camp. Start by hiking up the Parashant Canyon wash only a couple of hundred yards, then exit the wash on creek right and hike up into a small drainage past the basalt flow perched here. Stay on the trail and continue up to the ridgeline above you. You will need to skirt south into the next small draw to avoid a band of cliffs that cuts the ridge you are climbing up. Hike up to the top of this small draw to a saddle. Turn south and hike 100 yards to the base of a large limestone cliff. Skirt east a few hundred feet along this cliff and you will find a crack system that allows you to climb up into a small chute that cuts back to the west and to the top of the Redwall. At this point, you will need to find a way through one band of Supai before you top out on the Esplanade. Either proceed west-northwest one drainage and look for a broken section in the Supai cliff, or proceed up the closest ridge and take the Supai straight on. If you follow the ridge, with a little looking around, you will find a 20-foot chimney that gets you through the worst of the Supai. Hiking west to the top of the Supai band will offer your first view of the Nipple only 2 miles away.

From here, it's a straight walk toward the Nipple, with only an occasional small band of Supai sandstone boulders to negotiate. Mind that you protect the desert crust along the way. Hike right on up the east side of the Nipple's steep slope of Hermit Shale to the base of the Coconino sandstone cliffs. The route up through the Coconino is on the west side of this band of cliffs, so proceed around the north side to the west end. Look for a steep broken chimney on this side. This exposed chimney is the way up. At the top of this crack system you will need to walk up and around to the south on some narrow ledges, then back north up the last chute to the top. There is a fine view from the top of Mollies Nipple, north to the huge Andrus and Parashant Canyons, west to the eastern edge of the Shivwits Plateau, south to the Granite Park area, and west to Vulcan's Throne. The slice of river you can see is down by Spring Canyon. You are a long way from camp here, and will need to have taken some good mental notes to retrace your footsteps back to camp. Be sure to take enough food and munchies on this strenuous hike, and don't even think about it on a hot summer day.

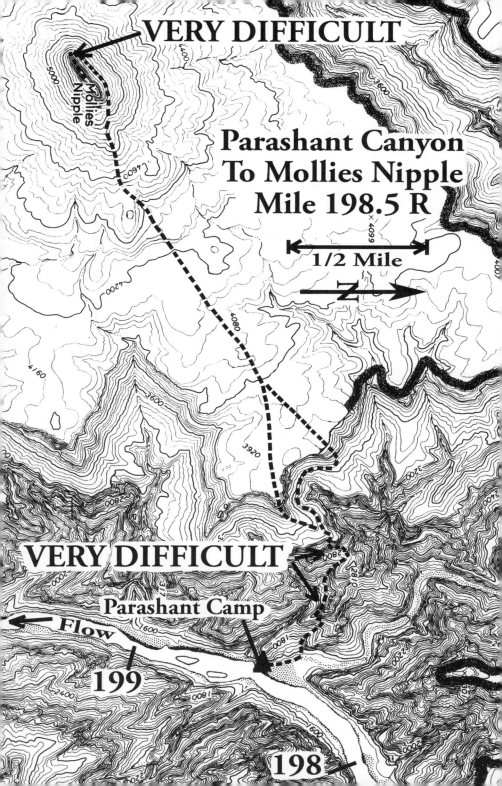

VERY DIFFICULT

Mollies Nipple

**Parashant Canyon
To Mollies Nipple
Mile 198.5 R**

1/2 Mile

N

VERY DIFFICULT

Parashant Camp

Flow

199

198

79. 202 Mile Canyon

Besides being a great place to camp, the pictographs, roasting pit and stone mortar at 202 make for a great and easy hike. There are two camps at 202, both on river right. The upper camp at Mile 201.9 R is just above the small riffle. It's an easy camp to miss. The popular lower camp at Mile 202.0 R is below the riffle and has a sandy beach running to a large basalt cliff at its downstream edge.

From either camp, you will want to walk northwest up the small wash behind camp. Only a few hundred yards along, the wash reaches a band of low limestone cliffs. To the north, look for a small path winding up to the base of the cliffs. Once at the cliff base, look around for some fine rock art. Some of the cliff has fallen away since the rock art was painted, so look for paintings at knee-height. This priceless treasure is relying on you and me to preserve it for the future. Remember, the oils on our hands will destroy these paintings if we touch them. There's a reason art is to be admired from afar.

On your way back to camp, look for a pile of burnt rock 30 feet or so in diameter. This is one of many agave roasting pits in this area of the Canyon. If you keep walking back toward the river through the debris fan created by this small wash, you may be lucky enough to find a smooth depression in one of the boulders. This smooth mortar is the business end of a grinding stone used by Puebloan Native Americans. As with all archaeological sites in Grand Canyon National Park, take only pictures, and don't even leave footprints if you can help it. This is a heavily visited site. If you see areas where brush is strategically placed in areas off the trail, that's where someone before you didn't remember to protect the desert soils, and wandered off to create another path. You can do your part to help preserve this wonderful canyon for future generations by staying on the path here.

202 Mile Canyon
Mile 201.9 R

1/4 Mile

N

Upper 202 Mile Camp

Rock Art

Lower 202 Mile Camp

Flow

202

80. Spring Canyon

One of the great things about Spring Canyon (Mile 204.4 R) is the water only 100 yards up this side canyon. When the main stem is running brown, clear water can be found here year-round. The pull-in is at the downstream end of a small eddy on river right, just above the Spring Canyon riffle. There may be running water from the spring right at the pull-in, but more often than not, you'll have to hike up the gravel wash a short distance before the water will appear. Some river parties have filled up their water containers and drunk the water right out of the creek without consequence, while others have run this water through their water treatment systems before drinking.

Besides water, 'you will need to be on the lookout for rattlesnakes in the spring, summer and fall. This little riparian oasis is host to a large assortment of lizards, toads and birds as well. The spring itself is another 50 to 100 yards up the wash, through thick brush, and comes bubbling out of the giant common reed Phragmites jungle in a number of spots. If you keep hiking up the wash, as soon as you are past the spring a dry, open canyon awaits your exploration.

There are some nice limestone narrows a few miles up Spring Canyon. To attempt the easy hike to the narrows, you will need to get past all the brush at the river. Once past that, it's easy going up the canyon. In just under 2 miles you will come to a major fork. Go right, or to the northwest. Another 1/2 mile or so takes you into the nice limestone narrows. This is not a fun hike if it's a hot day.

Another difficult hike here is to the top of the Redwall. You could do a layover at the small, brush-choked camp just below the riffle at Mile 204.5 R or camp at 202, float down and hike here, then go to 209 for the night. Any way you do it, you will need to get around the thick riverside vegetation and proceed 1/4 mile downriver from Spring Canyon to a small chute coming down to the river. Climb up the ridge on the south side of this chute. Continue on up this ridge through the broken Redwall. As you approach the very top of the Redwall, you will find traces of rock-work defining a stock trail. There is a large cairn at the top of the Redwall. Once at the top, hike back north to the point above Spring Canyon.

Here is another wonderful view of the heart of the western Grand Canyon region. Mollies Nipple is to the north, Dr. Tommy Mountain to the east across 205 Mile Canyon, and Granite Park is to the south. The Shivwits Plateau is the skyline to the west. The hike to the boats is as you came. It's very hot here in summer, with no shade unless you hike late in the day.

Spring Canyon
Mile 204.3 R

1/2 Mile

N

Spring

Canyon

Below Spring
Canyon Camp

203

Flow

204

205

81. 205 Mile Canyon

Two Hundred and Five Mile Canyon is a great place to go for an easy hike, though it's hot in the summer, as are most of the western Grand Canyon summer hikes. It's unique in that it's one of a few side canyons that allows you to hike through the Hurricane Fault. You'll want to pull in at the top of the rapid (Mile 205.4 L). This area gets late sun in the summer afternoon. You are entering Hualapai Nation land once you hike away from the river and will need a day-use permit to proceed.

There's no camp worth the name above the rapid. The nearest upstream camp is at Spring Canyon. A small group could try camping at the foot of the rapid on river left, but they would need to be sure to make the pull-in. Either way, you'll need to walk over to the wash that has made 205 Mile Rapid. Walk east up the wash away from the river. In less than 1/2 mile you will walk into some narrows. Within another 1/4 mile, the canyon opens up again on the east side of the fault, so it's easy to tell when you've walked right through the Hurricane Fault. Look for a small roasting pit on the north side of the creek in an overhang just before the creek turns northerly. In another 1/2 mile, the main arm of the drainage turns to the northeast.

From here, hikes are many. Bob Packard has hiked out through the Redwall in the northeast arm of the 205 Mile drainage on his way to the sky island above 209 Mile camp. Others have hiked the north arm toward 196 Mile Creek along the Hurricane Fault. Options, options. Remember, this is too toastie a place to be hiking in the hot time of the year.

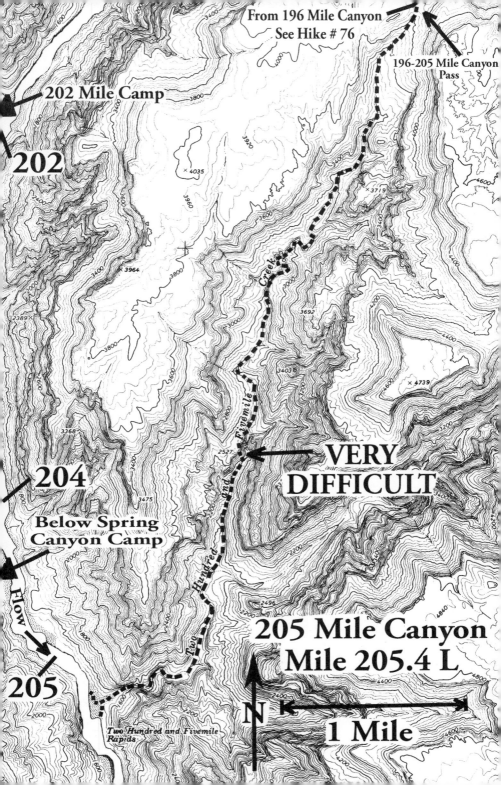

From 196 Mile Canyon
See Hike # 76

196-205 Mile Canyon
Pass

202 Mile Camp

202

204

Below Spring
Canyon Camp

205

Flow

**VERY
DIFFICULT**

**205 Mile Canyon
Mile 205.4 L**

N

1 Mile

Two Hundred and Fivemile
Rapids

82. Indian Canyon

There are a number of hikes at Indian Canyon, from short and easy to long and very difficult. Something is here for every hiker, even those who only want to hike from their camp chair to the boat and back. The camp here is at Mile 206.6 R. It's tucked into a back eddy, and is a nice small camp.

For a short hike to the Bundy Jars, look for the cairns on the north side of camp, and follow the trail as it winds its way up through broken Tapeats Sandstone cliffs a couple hundred yards, past an agave roasting pit, to a small cliff of Tapeats. There are a few glass jars here with odds and ends in them, attributed by some to have been placed here by the Bundies, a long-time Arizona Strip ranching family. That is questioned by long-time river runners who think the jars are more recent additions,, placed here by river runners. No matter, stay on the trail here to avoid damaging the fragile soils and plants.

The first of two difficult hikes is right on up the drainage. Okay, this one gets a very difficult rating. It's easy going for a mile, but then you will encounter a difficult pourover that you can get around on creek right. You can travel up a side draw 100 yards, then traverse back into the main drainage. In another 1/2 mile you will need to pass another pourover on creek right, then cross to creek left and work your way up out of the drainage to pass a major pourover, requiring some creative ledge work. Traverse back into the drainage. There's a very fine limestone-floored patio in the Redwall here, but alas, in another 1/3 mile a Supai chockstone blocks further travel. It's too bad too, because you are tantalizingly close to the top of the Redwall. The route back is as you have come.

The second difficult hike is a route up through the Redwall. This difficult hike has less exposure than the other very difficult hike, but has lots more elevation gain. It starts at the wash by the Bundy Jars and proceeds up the ridge to the southwest. This ridge goes high up into the Redwall. There will be some projecting spires to weave in and out through, but stay on the main ridgeline. Near the top of the Redwall, a level bench goes south 100 yards past a small overhang into a chute that goes to the top of the Redwall. From here you can walk 1/2 mile or less along the top of the Redwall to the southeast. It's broken in spots, but leads to a wonderful view. Mollies Nipple is to the north, as is camp. Dr. Tommy Mountain is to the east, the deep Redwall narrows of 209 are to the south and Price Point is to the west. It doesn't get much better than this. You will need water and food for these hikes, and a hat if it's warm. Don't try this if it's hot, as there's no shade anywhere. The way back is as you have come.

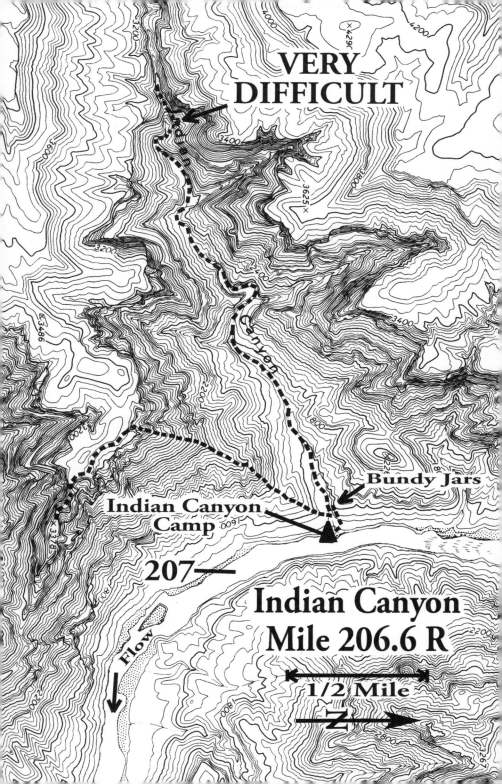

**VERY
DIFFICULT**

207

Bundy Jars

**Indian Canyon
Camp**

**Indian Canyon
Mile 206.6 R**

Flow

1/2 Mile

N

83. 209 Mile Canyon

Even though the walk up 209 Mile is an easy walk with some nice limestone narrows, it's a long walk through a hot canyon most of the year. The pull-in (Mile 208.75 R) is at the wash just above 209 Mile Rapid. The current moves past this wash, so be ready to get out and hold the boat unless you are ready to run 209 Mile Rapid on short notice.

From the pull-in, hike up the gradual gravel wash. It's 8 miles up to the Shivwits Plateau and Blue Mountain, but you might want to head for the nearest limestone narrows and get out of the heat. It's 2 1/2 miles or so up the wash to the first main fork in the drainage. Take the southern smaller fork, and in another 1/2 mile you will be in some nice limestone narrows. There is no water here, but it's a very quiet austere canyon, with its own beauty. The walk back to the boats is as you came.

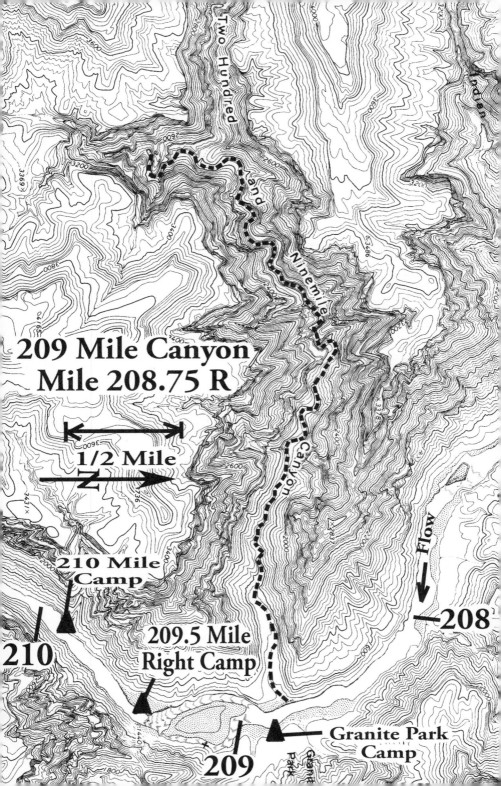

209 Mile Canyon
Mile 208.75 R

1/2 Mile

N

210 Mile
Camp

209.5 Mile
Right Camp

Granite Park
Camp

Flow

208

210

209

84. Granite Park

There is a lot to do at Granite Park, besides hanging out at a great camp and doing nothing but soaking up the winter sun or hanging in the shade on a hot summer day. The sweet-smelling blooms of many sand verbenas make this a heavenly camp in mid- to late-March. Hikes include going south up a difficult route to the top of the Redwall and west up a very difficult route to Dr. Tommy Mountain, which is the unofficial name J.D. Green uses for this sky island. Smithson and Euler, in their book Havasupai Legends, note that Dr. Tommy was a Hualapai shaman in the early 1900s. All hikes from here are in the Hualapai Nation and you will need a day-use permit to hike away from the river. The pull-in for this camp is at Mile 208.8 L. There is a large eddy on river left at the top of 209 Mile Rapid. You will need to swing along shore and pull in at the sandy opening about halfway along this eddy.

As with all camps, I try to avoid creating new trails, and avoid using old multiple trails that are being revegetated. This camp can use our help to stay free of trash.

To hike south to the Esplanade, proceed downriver and onto the small ridge that runs north-south and starts just south of the Granite Park Canyon wash. Hike onto the top of this ridge and south up-slope into the limestone buttress clearly visible from camp. Work your way up through the broken cliffs, using the many chutes to continue climbing up. There is a small bit of easy chimney work right at the top, but you have only come a little over a mile from camp. Once you top out, hike 1/2 mile or so west to the point of Esplanade here. There is a great view of the river below, the Shivwits Plateau to the west, Granite Park Canyon to the east and Dr. Tommy to the north. The route back to camp is as you came.

Dr. Tommy Mountain is a mile above the Granite Park camp and only 2 1/2 miles distant (in a straight line of sight), but don't let that fool you. This hike takes all day, and is the equal in elevation gain to hiking from Phantom Ranch up the Kaibab Trail to the rim and back, except there is NO trail. This hike is a winter hike.

To attempt to climb Dr. Tommy, hike upriver from camp to the first wash coming in from the east. Hike up this wash about a mile into a Redwall basin with sheer cliffs to the north and east, and a broken ridge to the south. Hike southeast 1/2 mile to the top of this ridge, where a small saddle separates the drainage you have just hiked up from the northernmost tributary of the Granite Park drainage.

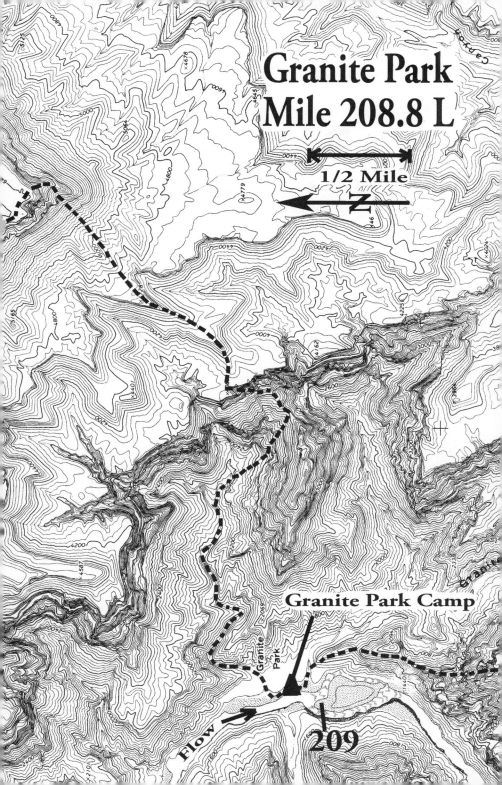

Granite Park
Mile 208.8 L

1/2 Mile

N

Granite Park Camp

Granite Park

Flow

209

84. Granite Park contd.

From this saddle you will be able to see what you could not see before, which is the precious view of a small chute going back to the north up through the Redwall. Traverse over to the chute from the saddle and climb up the chute to the top of the Redwall. You might want to hike the few yards over to the Redwall edge and take in the view from here.

Looming to the north and east of you is Dr Tommy Mountain. Hike northeast through a ridge of low Supai cliffs toward the southernmost corner of Dr. Tommy. This corner is a steep slope going right on up through the Hermit Shale into broken Coconino Sandstone. You will have to do a little route-finding up through the ridge of Coconino, but it's easy to find a way. Another slope of Toroweap, and some broken cliffs of Kaibab are easily hiked through to the top. You are a mile high here, having hiked about 4 miles from camp.

To really appreciate where you are, hike over the Moenkopi (that's right) west through the Pinion and juniper along the rim another 1 1/2 miles to the southwest corner of the mountain. You are close to the "official" summit here, but this flat-topped mountain has no well-defined peak. Yes, that is Diamond Peak to the south, with the Aubery Cliffs east of Peach Springs in the distance. To the northwest is Mount Dellenbaugh.

Considering the chances of your being here again, and given enough daylight left, you might want to go the extra mile north to get the view from the western-most corner of Dr. Tommy. From here you have an impressive view down into the 205 Mile drainage, and on a clear day you can see all the way to the Pine Valley Mountains just north of St. George, Utah. This is undoubtedly one of the western hearts of Grand Canyon. You are a long way from camp here, so don't stay too long. You will need to be out all day on this hike, with enough food and water to keep your batteries well-charged. There is no shade on this hike except what you bring with you.

85. Pumpkin Spring

Pumpkin Springs, at Mile 212.9 L, has a couple of fun attractions. The pull-in is below the dome-shaped spring on river left. The big dune camp here used to be a popular one, but has become very small in recent years. The spring is high in natural arsenic, so consider a bath at your own risk.

There's an interesting spot in some Tapeats ledges 1/8 mile back upriver. To get there, hike upriver along the top of the Tapeats. This bench used to be scoured by high floodwaters before Glen Canyon Dam checked the cycle of seasonal flooding in 1963. If you walk along the edge of the Tapeats, you will find a circular hole about 3- to 4-feet-wide going straight down 6 or 7 feet to a small ledge, This ledge takes you out over the river and back to the Tapeats top. Be careful along the edge, as a fall into the river could be fatal. This is a fun place to explore on a hot summer day, as the Tapeats Sandstone stays cool near the river water. The return is as you have come.

86. The Snyder Cabin

Just across the river and downstream 1/8 mile from Pumpkin Spring is the remains of a prospectors' cabin, attributed to miners who worked the Snyder Mine up 214 Mile Canyon (see hike # 87). To spot this cabin from Pumpkin Spring, look across the river. You will see a talus slope coming down from the Redwall. There are three out-crops of dark-reddish-brown Bright Angel Shale all on the same level jutting through the slope. Between the middle one and the upstream one is a small, year-round seep. These outcrops are maybe 200 feet above the river. The cabin site is at the base of the middle outcrop. There is a chimney at the site, clearly visible from the river, but, as it's built of the same dark-reddish-brown Bright Angel Shale, it's hard to spot. The river makes a wide big pool at Pumpkin Springs, then gathers up in a very small riffle and heads on downstream. To get to the Snyder Cabin, enter this riffle and pull to shore at Mile 213.0 R. Look for the cairns leading up a talus pile to the south side of the cabin site. Stay on the trail here, going up through the boulder pile 100 yards or so. The trail crew built this trail up the hillside following a very old debris flow, so most of the trail is up a rockslide. You can see some of their stonework if you look hard. At the cabin site you'll find a few small glass bottles, tin cans and other odds and ends from the 1920s and 30s. This is an open air museum so don't touch, take pictures, and leave everything where you find it and as you find it. Go back as you came up.

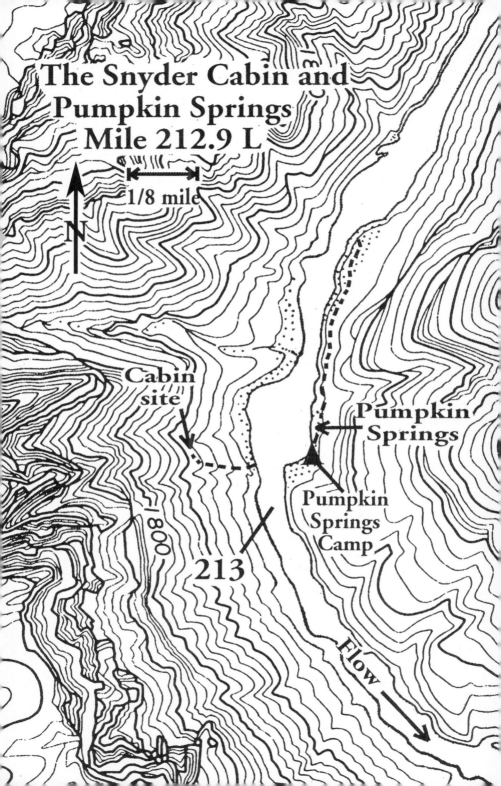

The Snyder Cabin and
Pumpkin Springs
Mile 212.9 L

1/8 mile

N

Cabin
site

Pumpkin
Springs

Pumpkin
Springs
Camp

800

213

Flow

87. 214 Mile Canyon

A great camp (Mile 214.3 R) and long, difficult hike up an old stock trail to the top of the Redwall and Shanley Spring make 214 Mile Canyon an interesting place to explore in the fall, spring or winter. There is good noon shade at this camp for a summer lunch siesta, but searching for shade is about all you will want to do here in the summertime. The pull-in for this camp is at the bottom of the debris fan formed by the next drainage 100 yards or so below the riffle formed by 214 Mile Canyon. Look for a sandy beach with a Tapeats cliff at its back, with overhangs in the cliff providing shade in the noonday sun, and shelter from a monsoon storm.

The hike from 214 is long and often hot, even in the winter. To start this hike, you will need to go up through the Tapeats cliff behind camp, at the top of the debris fan by a small dry waterfall. Once on top of the Tapeats cliff, walk northwest 1/4 mile, skirting the west side of a large perched flow of basalt, leaving the small drainage behind camp and entering into the 214 Mile drainage. Contour on a level route into the normally dry 214 Mile creekbed. There may be a few small seeps here with a little water after a wet winter.

From here, hike 1 1/2 miles up the creekbed. Expect to do some boulder hopping along the way and to encounter one pourover that you will have to climb straight up through. You will finally reach a pourover that will stop your forward progress. At this point, leave the creekbed and follow the trail climbing up the talus slope on creek right. At the top of this talus slope, rock-work signals that you are on the 214 Mile trail. This trail leads up through the cliff above the pourover below, and contours back into the drainage above the falls. The trail is overgrown in spots, but winds its way for 1/2 mile up and out of the main 214 Mile drainage through a wide break in the Redwall, which pinches to a narrow chute near its top. The trail, with visible rock-work, switchbacks up through this chute to the top of the Redwall. From here, hike west a few hundred yards into a small drainage, then turn and head up the ridge to the south. Continue south and in 1/2 mile you will see a small butte. The Snyder copper mine is on the south side of this butte, another 1/4 mile along.

**214 Mile Canyon
Mile 214.2 R**

1/2 Mile

214 Mile Camp

214

87. 214 Mile Canyon contd.

To hike to Shanley Spring, head south 3/4 mile from the Snyder Mine into the headwaters of Trail Canyon. Follow the drainage downstream into the top of the Redwall to a pourover you will not be able to climb down, with a limestone cliff on your right. Leave the drainage on the creek right side, following the top of this limestone cliff for a hundred yards or so. You will come to 75 yards worth of trail with rock-work traversing down through this cliff face. Some of the old trail has fallen away, and the ledge that is left is rather narrow. Follow the trail into the drainage. At the bottom of the cliff you have just hiked through, near the base of the pourover, is a lone juniper tree. Hike over and up the short climb to the tree. Behind it, surprise surprise, is a small clear pool of water with a few cattails growing at the pool's edge. There is a small seep in the back of this pool dripping cool clear water off a travertine stalactite. It's only 3 1/2 miles back to the boats from here via the way you got here, but it's a long way. Be sure to bring enough water on this hike, and pack a lunch. There is no shade up here, and it's amazingly hot here in the early spring and late fall.

88. Three Springs Canyon

Three Springs Canyon offers much for the Canyon traveler: shade at the river on a hot summer day, clear water nearby, and opportunities for some great easy hiking. There is no camp here, though. The pull-in is just before Three Springs Rapid at Mile 215.6 L. Look for a band of 50-foot-high cliffs on river left, and pull in to the small eddy just above these cliffs. There is a 100-yard-or-so-long trail here up and over the cliffs to the permanent stream at the mouth of the canyon. Some trips have filled their water jugs here without treating the water, while others prefer to treat the water they collect here.

You are entering Hualapai Nation land once you hike away from the river and will need a day-use permit to proceed. The hiker will find that the Three Springs water source is in heavy brush within 1/4 mile of the Colorado. Beyond the spring, a dry, open (hot in the summer) wash is easily followed for at least 2 miles west toward the east rim of the Grand Canyon. At this point, the rim is only 4 miles as the crow flies and over 4000 feet overhead. There are multiple side canyons in Three Springs Canyon, with many hiking opportunities. Of interest is the fact that the start of the Prospect Canyon drainage, responsible for Lava Falls, is right on the other side of the east-rim skyline.

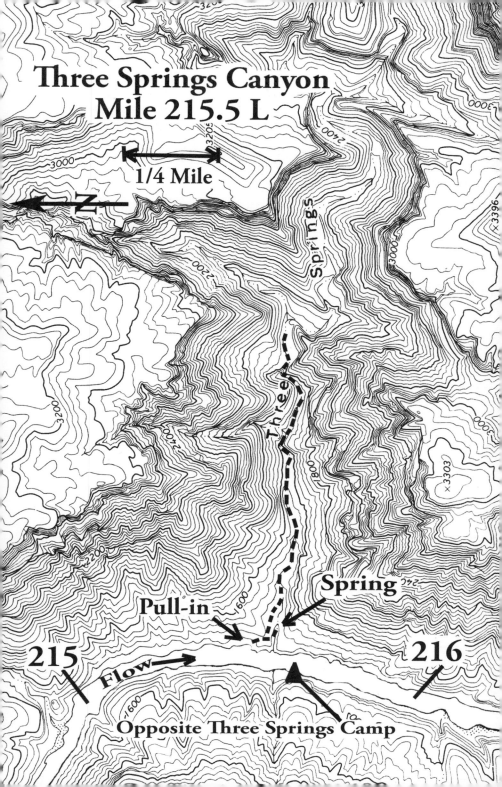

Three Springs Canyon
Mile 215.5 L

1/4 Mile

N

Springs

Three

Spring

Pull-in

215

216

Flow

Opposite Three Springs Camp

89. 220 Mile Canyon

There are three popular "last night" camps at 220 Mile Canyon (Mile 219.8 R), with an easy and a difficult hike as well. The lowest camp has first shade, but is the smallest of the three, and getting smaller as the beach washes away. The upper camp has the second best shade, while the biggest camp with the latest afternoon summer sun is the middle camp. These are popular summertime "last night on the river" camps, so if you don't want to camp with others around who may be partying, you may want to take this into your campsite consideration. This is another camp to pay special attention to keeping clean. Actually, all canyon camps need you to help keep them clean.

First the easy hike. There is a fine enjoyable stroll up the 220 Mile wash into a schist and Tapeats narrows canyon. The geologists will tell you it's not Schist but the Diamond Creek Pluton, but never mind. There is a small seep in the wash less than 1/2 mile from camp, and in this area the wash bed is a very impressive jumble of conglomerate boulders that have been polished smooth by the force of the water during flash floods. It's worth the walk up to look at this smooth polished conglomerate.

The difficult hike starts at the first (upriver) camp. It's about 2 miles round trip, and requires some steep scrambling. Head out of camp to the northwest, hiking up the draw from camp in this direction. You will see a way through the Tapeats cliffs where a small fault has broken the cliff down. Once onto the top of the Tapeats, hike overland to the north-northwest, heading into Trail Canyon. In 1/2 mile, you will reach a fine viewpoint where you can look down into Trail Canyon from the top of the Tapeats. Unless Trail Canyon has recently flash-flooded, there will be a lot of vegetation with a permanent trickle of water in the canyon floor. If you look at the bed of Trail Canyon, you can pick out the outlines of an old prospectors' camp. Smart folks will turn back here.

If you want to hike to this old camp, hike along the top of the Tapeats cliffs farther into Trail Canyon. In about 1/4 mile, there is a break in the Tapeats, and a slope drops into the bottom of the canyon. It's an easy backtrack down the creekbed to the camp. Please leave the bits of rusted metal alone at this open-air museum. The return route is via the way you came. If you get the bright idea of walking down Trail Canyon to the river, and then hiking back along the river edge to camp, please think again. It's pretty enough and fairly easy to get down the creekbed to the river, but the 1/2 mile from the mouth of Trail Canyon to 220 is sheer hell. Steep granite drops right into the river, and Tapeats cliffs keep you from topping back out above them. Why mess up a good evening stroll? Be smart and head back the way you came.

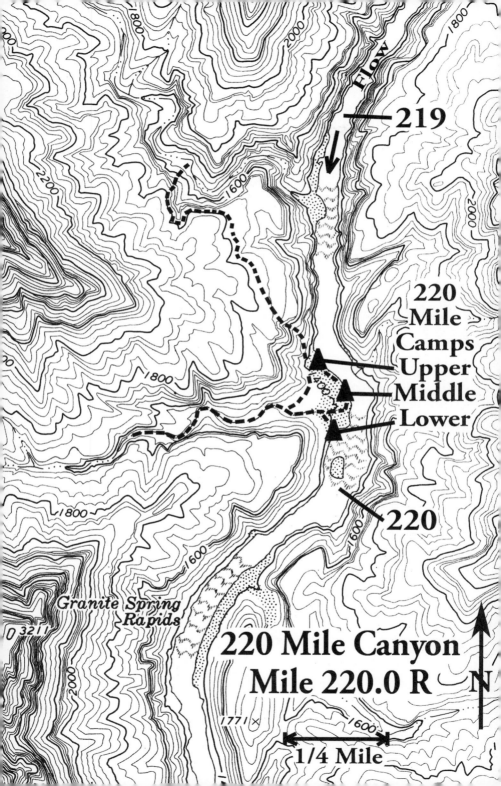

Flow

219

220
Mile
Camps
Upper
Middle
Lower

220

Granite Spring
Rapids

0 3211

1771 ×

220 Mile Canyon
Mile 220.0 R

N

1/4 Mile

90. 222 Mile Canyon

One of the really enjoyable west-end camps is here at 222 Mile Canyon at Mile 222.0 L. The pull-in is straightforward, as there are large eddies on river left and right, with slow current in the middle of the river. This camp has verbena in the spring filling the morning air with a sweet smell. Evening sunsets are fine here too. If you want to have a quiet last night on the river, this is your camp.

Okay, so how about hiking from here? You bet. You are entering Hualapai Nation land once you hike away from the river and will need a day-use permit to proceed. There are a couple of easy options of 1 to 2 miles. Both start in the drainage behind camp. For a short stroll, head up the drainage. In 1/2 mile or so you will come to a small seep spring in the schist. It's a pleasant stroll. For a longer hike, head up the drainage 1/4 mile from camp and look for a small drainage entering from the northeast. Head up this drainage a little under 1/2 mile. The geologists in your group will recognize the exposed faulting of the rock here in the drainage bottom. This is an extension of the Hurricane Fault (see hike # 81). You will crest a small saddle at the top of this drainage, then traverse northwest through a few broken bands of cliffs to crest the summit of a small unnamed butte.

This is a really enjoyable hike on a cloudy day, or any day it's not too hot. The view from this little butte is very precious. Diamond Peak dominates the southern skyline with the river winding past it. To the west is 220 Mile Canyon. To the north is the mesa between Trail and 214 Mile Canyons. Dr. Tommy Mountain dominates the northern skyline. This is a wonderful sunset spot.

202

222 Mile Canyon
Mile 222.0 L

1/4 Mile

N

221

221 Mile Camp

Flow

222 Mile Camp

222

91. Diamond Peak from 224 Mile Canyon

224 Mile camp, the start for this hike, is just above 224 Mile Rapid at Mile 223.4 L. There's a strong eddy here on river left, just above 224 Mile Rapid. You may have to work a little at catching the reverse eddy in the downstream corner-pocket pull-in. You are entering Hualapai Nation land once you hike away from the river and will need a day-use permit to proceed. The route to Diamond Peak goes up the wash just downstream from camp that makes the rapid you are camping above. Look for a nice trickle of water here in the early spring months. Follow this drainage up to the first tributary coming in on your right (from the south) and follow the route up this wash to the Diamond Peak saddle. Follow the path here and avoid multiple trailing.

This easy walk should take you an hour or two. Remember, in the heat of a summer day you don't want to do this hike. A cloudy monsoon afternoon or a winter day makes this a pleasant walk. From the saddle you can see south into the Peach Springs drainage, with the winding Diamond Creek Road in it. To the north is the sky island outside of Granite Park. This is a good place to turn back, unless you want to climb Diamond Peak, are not troubled by very difficult hikes with exposure, and find scrambling over loose rock easy.

To continue to the top of Diamond Peak, you will need to proceed west from the saddle, up the ridge to a broken wall of limestone. There is a small broken chute leading up to a twisting ridge walk-up to the top. This route is exposed, with loose-clothes-and skin-tearing Redwall all the way. Once at the top, you will have a fine view of the Canyon to the north, with the Granite Park sky island Dr. Tommy Mountain dominating the skyline. The view west is to Kelly Point, and there is a view down the Canyon to the Travertine Canyon drainage. The view here is sublime. You'll need the same supplies as always, food and water, and a half-day should be more than enough to get you to the top and back.

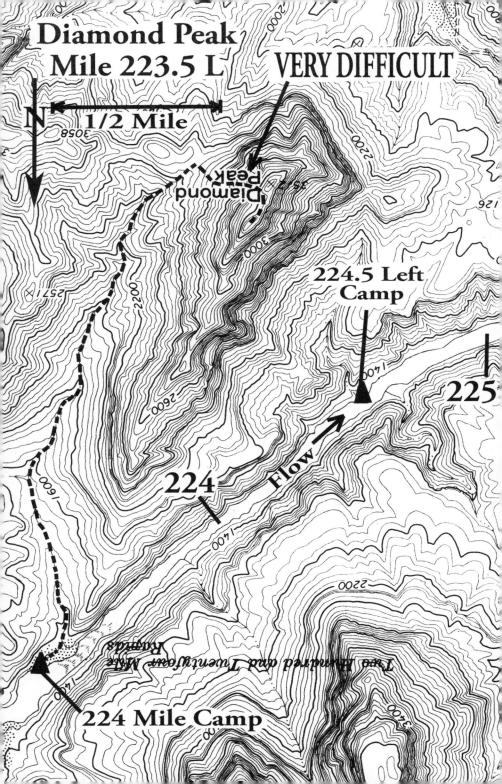

Diamond Peak
Mile 223.5 L

VERY DIFFICULT

N

|← 1/2 Mile →|

Diamond Peak

224.5 Left
Camp

225

Flow

224

1600

224 Mile Camp

Two Hundred and Twentyfour Mile Rapids

92. Diamond Creek

Diamond Creek offers much more than just a take-out point to end your river trip. From an easy hike to a nice waterfall, to a difficult hike far into western Grand Canyon with water to boot, this drainage has some great excursions.

The upper pull-in at Diamond Creek is fairly straightforward. There is a flat water run of almost 2 miles below 224 Mile Rapid. A small riffle at 225.5 signals the approach of Diamond Creek, as does the noise from Diamond Creek Rapid at Mile 225.8. If you are going to day hike only, you will want to pull in well above the boat ramp, at Mile 225.6 L. As you approach the Diamond Creek debris fan, look for a small wooden catwalk bolted to the granite cliff just upstream from the fan. This is used by the USGS river flow gauge workers. As soon as this granite cliff meets the debris fan, there is a small break in the riverside brush. You will want to get into the river left eddy here to pull in. If you are taking out at Diamond Creek, you will want to row down to the boat ramp just 75 yards or so downstream at Mile 225.7 L. Please note that it is very easy to miss this pull-in if other boats are at the take-out. If you get swept into Diamond Creek Rapid, plan on adding a lot of hard work to your take-out plans.

For an easy 2-mile walk to a nice waterfall, hike up the Diamond Creek Road, which fords the permanent water in Diamond Creek a number of times. In roughly a mile, the Diamond Creek Road heads south into Peach Spring Canyon. Leave the road and follow the flowing brook on up Diamond Creek another mile. The creek makes a large sweep to the left, then back around to your right in a large goose-neck. At the end of this goose neck, you have crossed the Hurricane Fault and are now back into the Vishnu Schist. The canyon narrows considerably and quickly at this point. You will find a wonderful waterfall here, 7 or 8 feet high, in deep shade. This is a great place for a quick dip in the summertime.

Following the watercourse farther requires difficult scrambling. Continue on up past the narrows into the broad open Diamond Creek valley. Unless the creek has recently flashed, the going can be very brushy. I have only been another 3 1/2 miles beyond the waterfall, to the junction of Diamond Creek and the dry Blue Mountain Canyon. From here, it's another 3 1/2 and 4 1/2 miles to the two Diamond Creek springs. The walking in Diamond Creek gets more brushy beyond the junction with Blue Mountain Canyon. Please note that Diamond Creek is known for its plentiful supply of rattlesnakes and small biting gnats. This is a great place to hike in the winter when both populations are mostly dormant. You are entering Hualapai Nation land once you hike away from the river and will need a day-use permit to proceed.

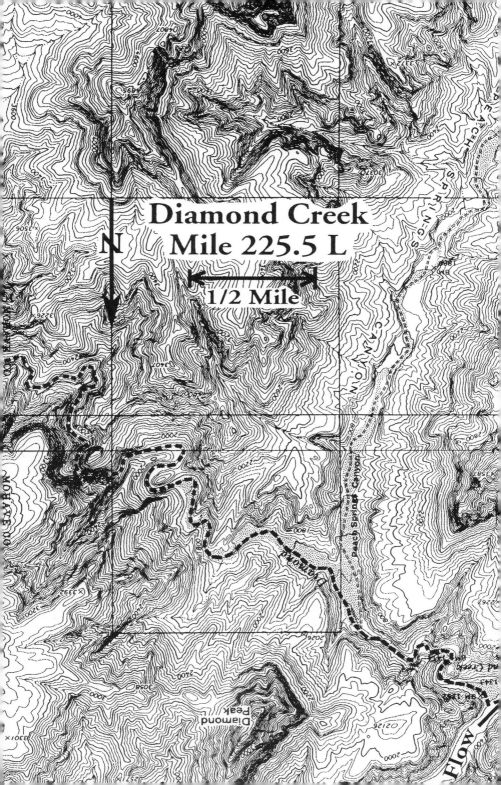

Diamond Creek
Mile 225.5 L

N

1/2 Mile

93. Travertine Canyon

Travertine Canyon is interesting for its combination of beauty and danger. There is a small, heavily used bouldery camp on the Travertine Canyon debris fan, and a very difficult hike to a fantastic waterfall right next to the river. There is also a very difficult hike into the streambed above the waterfall, with a 2-mile walk from the river to the source spring.

There are two camps that access Travertine Canyon. The upper camp is very small (Mile 228.9+ L) and is at the drainage just above Travertine Rapid. There is a scramble of less than 1/4 mile along slippery schist cliffs at water's edge to get down to Travertine Canyon from this camp. The lower camp (Mile 229.0 L) has a hard pull-in. Stay on the left side of the river, and be ready to catch the micro-eddy at the foot of the rapid. The camp is the boulder pile beside this eddy. There are spots to set down a bedroll if you look, and are willing to share with a few red ants. The better you keep your camp clean, the higher the chances the ants will need to forage for food up away from camp.

The series of waterfalls behind camp is very impressive, both for their evaporative cooling effect in the summer and the need for good climbing skills to climb up the slick hot schist at the mouth of the biggest falls if you want to reach them. The first waterfall you encounter is a nice place to hang out if you don't want to practice your spider-like climbing techniques. If you want to climb farther, the creek-left side offers a possibility to continue, if you stay 30 feet above the streambed and traverse across a steep slippery slope above the second waterfall. If you manage this, then there is a third waterfall you climb past, again on the creek-left side. At the top of this small fall is a 100-foot-or-so section of gravel-bottomed creekbed, leading into a travertine slot canyon, with cool shade and a thundering waterfall at its back.

A good climber can free climb the dry chute on the creek left side of the waterfall and walk across the chock boulder wedged in the top of the narrows to get back into the creekbed for more exploring. Alternatively, climb up the hillside just upriver and across the streambed from camp. There is a small path that goes up this slope, then traverses back and drops down into the stream above all of these waterfalls. There are some tight schist narrows with a few difficult waterfalls to climb, but the dedicated climber can continue on. Within a mile from the river, the going gets easier, and the streambed turns into a gravel wash and heads up an open valley to the southwest. In another mile, the spring is reached, where a large amount of water emerges out of the ground in a Phragmites jungle. The route back is as you came. Exercise extreme caution while climbing by the falls; many accidents have occurred here. You are entering Hualapai Nation land once you hike away from the river and will need a day-use permit to proceed.

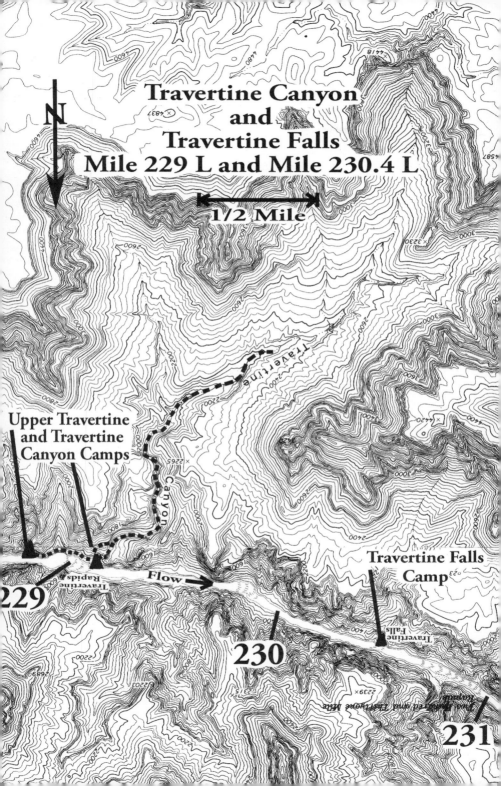

Travertine Canyon
and
Travertine Falls
Mile 229 L and Mile 230.4 L

← 1/2 Mile →

N

Travertine

Upper Travertine
and Travertine
Canyon Camps

Canyon

Travertine Rapids

Flow →

Travertine Falls
Camp

Travertine Falls

229

230

231

94. Travertine Falls

There is a small camp on river left at Mile 230.5 L, with a nice trickle of water cascading over a broad travertine fan called Travertine Falls. If you are going to camp here, scout around, as sometimes the camp 100 yards below the falls is better, and sometimes the one 50 yards above is the better one. This depends on river flow and sand deposition. Either way, it's a very easy stroll over to the base of the falls. There is summer shade here, as this is a north-facing waterfall.

Peter Dayton tells me that you can scramble straight up through the schist here and get up on the Tapeats Sandstone, which in this section forms a nice terrace like the Tonto Platform in the upper Canyon. It's very hot here in the summertime.

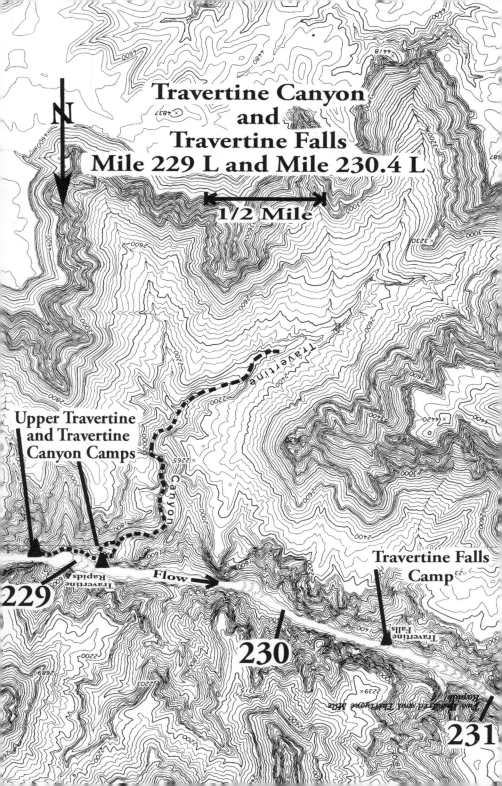

Travertine Canyon
and
Travertine Falls
Mile 229 L and Mile 230.4 L

1/2 Mile

N

Upper Travertine
and Travertine
Canyon Camps

Travertine Falls
Camp

Travertine Rapids

Flow

Travertine Falls

229

230

231

Two Hundred and Thirtyone Mile
Rapids

95. Bridge Canyon

There is a great little camp tucked away at Bridge Canyon (Mile 235.25 L), and a fine easy walk to the conglomerate bridge that gives this canyon its name. The camp is in the middle of the rapid, with a pull-in right at the top of the rapid, and a hard pull-in at the foot of the rapid. To make the lower pull-in, you will need to be on river left as you enter the rapid, and be ready to pull hard to the left shore to catch the small eddy at the foot of the rapid. You can always scout it out from the top of the rapid if you are unsure about it. This camp is one of those tucked-away spots you'll be glad to find. It is a loud camp with the roar of Bridge Canyon Rapid never-ending.

From camp, there is a small path leading up into Bridge Canyon. The path stays on the creek-left side of the canyon for the most part, but will cross the streambed and travel up the flowing brook for a ways. There is a permanent spring here with a small stream in the canyon bottom with lots of vegetation. The bridge is less than 1/2 mile from the river at a point where the canyon turns hard to the west. Look for the bridge at this bend a few hundred feet up a small side drainage on creek right. It's easy to miss if you are not looking for it. As with the rest of the far west end of Grand Canyon, this is an oven in the summer. You are entering Hualapai Nation land once you hike away from the river and will need a day-use permit to proceed. I try to stay on the path to avoid damaging the riparian vegetation here, and count on all river runners to help keep this heavily used camp clean.

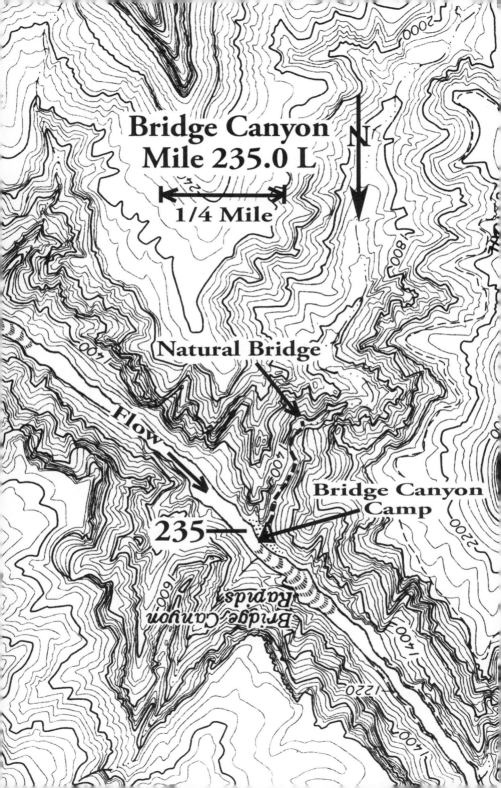

Bridge Canyon
Mile 235.0 L

1/4 Mile

N

Natural Bridge

Flow

Bridge Canyon
Camp

235

Bridge Canyon Rapids

96. Bridge City

Just above Separation Canyon, the remains of the proposed Bridge Canyon Dam and Bridge City can be found. Bridge City Camp, at river mile 238.5 on river left, is a small, brushy camp at Bridge City. Remains of the dam builders' camp at Bridge City are visible here as well. Rock foundations, steel cable, piping and other bits of steel are still scattered about this area.

The actual dam site location was just upstream of Bridge City. As you approach Bridge City, be on the lookout for signs of exploration conducted in the 1940s through 1950s for the proposed Bridge Canyon Dam between river mile 237.5 and 238. In this area on river right, look for a 4' x 5' wooden door placed in front of an overhang in the schist which at one time provided a location to store dynamite. On river left, the remains of a wooden table with the occasional piece of steel drilling equipment may be spotted. Exploratory openings into the schist are also evident here on both sides of the river.

The 740 foot Bridge Canyon Dam would have raised the water level 672 feet to a maximum elevation of 1,876 feet above sea level. The impoundment would have extended upstream 93 miles to within less then a half mile of the mouth of Kanab Creek.

This dam construction was stopped in the end by Public Law 93-620, the Grand Canyon National Park Enlargement Act. President Ford signed this bill into law in 1975. Jeff Ingram and John McComb, who throughout most of the late 1960s and early 1970s, fought hard to keep this area dam-free. Our thanks go to these two for Matkatamiba, Havasu, Tuckup, Lava Falls, 202 Mile, Granite Park, Diamond Creek, Travertine Grotto and Falls, 232 Mile Rapid, and everything else between here and Kanab.

There is a nice short easy hike here up to the top of the Tapeats with a good view. You are entering Hualapai Nation land once you hike away from the river and will need a day-use permit to proceed. From Bridge City, hike south southwest up the small drainage visible from camp. In just under a quarter mile, you will crest the top of the Tapeats. Walk northeast a couple of hundred yards to a very fine overlook of the river to the east and north. Can you envision a 700 foot-high dam here? The route down is as you have come.

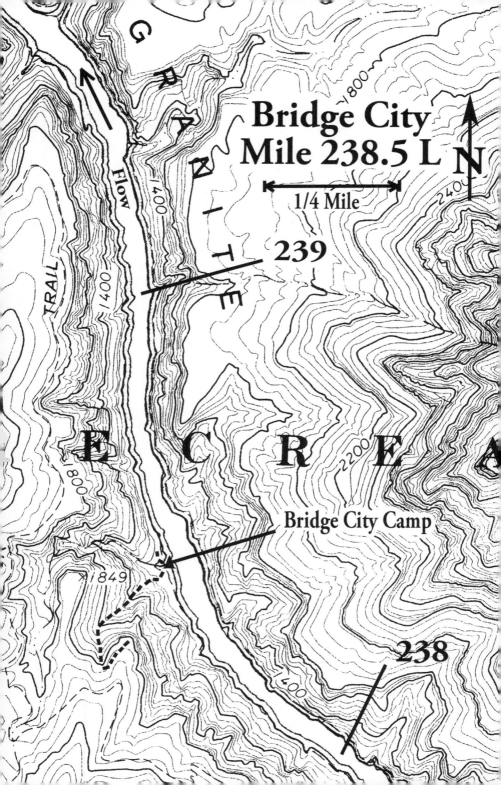

**Bridge City
Mile 238.5 L**

1/4 Mile

239

Bridge City Camp

238

GRANITE

Flow

TRAIL

E C R E A

N

97. Separation Canyon

Separation Canyon, at Mile 239.6 R, is a rough camp unless the water level in Lake Mead is low. A river buoy marks the limit to upstream travel at this point. If you pull in on the downstream side of Separation Canyon, you can check out the camping scene, and take in a couple of easy hikes. There is a historic cenotaph just above this pull-in for the two Howland Brothers, O.G. and Seneca, and William Dunn, who in the summer of 1896 decided to hike away from trip leader John Wesley Powell's rafting party. It is possible to hike out Separation Canyon; but the Howlands and Dunn were never seen again. Pioneer settlers on the Shivwits Plateau may have killed them. The marker noting this event is just 70 feet above the beach here, and it is an easy hike up through the schist to reach it.

Separation Canyon is a fault-controlled canyon and runs for 2 1/2 miles more or less straight before the first substantial fork. I have not been beyond this first fork. There is water in the gravel wash bottom most years, which makes for enjoyable walking. There is a lot of Tamarisk at the mouth of the Canyon you will have to work your way through for the first 100 yards or so as you hike away from the river. This southwest-trending canyon is wide enough to have full-on sun year-round, which makes hiking here in the summer brutal.

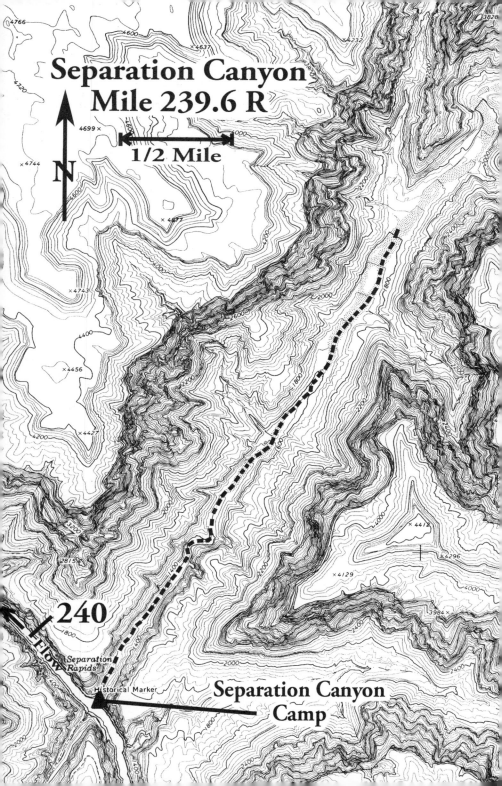

Separation Canyon
Mile 239.6 R

N

1/2 Mile

240

FLOW

Separation
Rapids

Historical Marker

Separation Canyon
Camp

98. 242 Mile Canyon

Just because the rapids are behind you doesn't mean you are no longer surrounded by great hiking. The camp at 242 Mile Canyon is just the thing for some easy, difficult, and very difficult hiking. The camp for hiking 242 is called 243 Mile and is at Mile 242.8 R, tucked away at the foot of a small bay. This camp, also known as "Bob's Birthday Camp" for lontime river runner Bob Flamme, is a great camp in a location where great camps are few and far between.

For a short, easy hike of less than 1 mile, hike north out of camp, following a small path into the drainage, then follow it up and to the north from camp. In less than 1/4 mile you will top a small saddle. Hike 1/4 mile west out to a high bluff overlooking the drowned river a few hundred feet below. There is a fine view of the canyon to the east and south. The return is as you have come.

For a difficult hike, drop down the chute on the north side of the saddle into 242 Mile Canyon. The difficult part of this hike is this chute. Once you reach the floor of 242 Mile, it's an easy walk north for 1 1/2 miles up this gravel wash to a limestone patio at the junction of the north and east arms of 242. You could call it good here and head on back the way you have come.

But, should you like to attempt the very difficult route through the Redwall, head to the west side of the north drainage. You will see a ridge trending northwest and going quite a ways up to the base of the Redwall. You will need to work this ridge northeast and southwest as you climb it to pick your way through broken bands of 50- to 100–foot-high cliffs along the way. There is no climbing involved here if you switchback your way up this ridge to the base of the Redwall proper. From here, hike north 1/4 mile to a very small ramp that leads up into the Redwall cliff. You will now see a broken steep slope. Switchback your way up this slope to the base of a chute going up and to the west. This chute will go to the top of a ridge leading north and through the last of the Redwall. From the top of the Redwall, you might want to hike to the north less than a mile, skirting a small bay on your way, to a ridge between Surprise Canyon to the west and 242 Mile Canyon to the east.

There's quite the view up here. The deeply entrenched Surprise Canyon is to your west, with Twin Point to the north, Mount Dellenbaugh to the northeast, Amos point to the west and the great sweep of Grand Canyon to the south. You are a long way from camp, with the way back the same way you came to get here. You will need food and water for a day to hike this route. This is not a summer hike. Hike on durable surfaces to protect the native vegetation and soil.

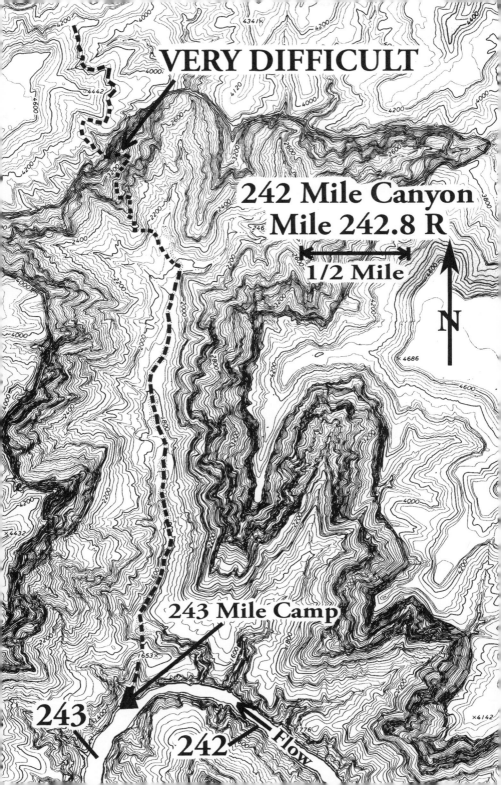

VERY DIFFICULT

**242 Mile Canyon
Mile 242.8 R**

1/2 Mile

N

243 Mile Camp

243

242

Flow

99. Burnt Springs

The Burnt Springs area offers some fine hiking opportunities, and a great camp when Lake Mead is close to full pool. Camp is on river right (Mile 259.5 R) just above the huge Burnt Springs Canyon bay. Look for a band of low limestone cliffs, 15-feet-high at full pool, right at the upstream corner of the bay. Tie up where a small path comes down to the water's edge. You will find a flat bench at the top of this cliff that makes for a very nice camp. There are remnants of an old shack nearby.

Just across the river from camp and downstream 1/2 mile is the mouth of Quartermaster Canyon. There is a large hillside deposit of travertine on river left here, built up from calcium carbonate leaching out of the spring water. The spring at Burnt Springs has since changed to a new discharge point, but climbing up onto the flat mesa formed by the spring is a good half-hour walk. You can see the old entrenched streambed on the mesa's top where the spring water used to flow. On the Quartermaster Canyon side of the river, you are entering Hualapai Nation land once you hike away from the river and will need a day-use permit to proceed.

This area is also the landing zone for helicopter tours out of McCarin Airport in Las Vegas. The helicopters don't take too kindly to your looking up at them open-mouthed, especially if you are standing in the middle of their landing pad.

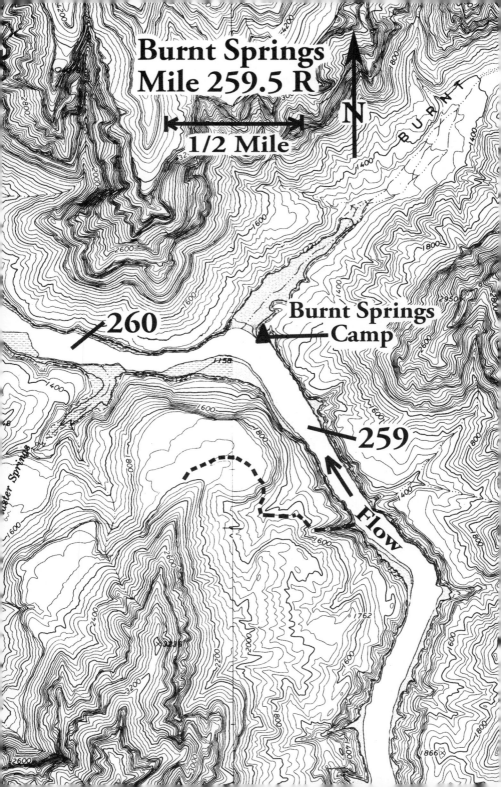

Burnt Springs
Mile 259.5 R

N

1/2 Mile

260

Burnt Springs
Camp

259

Flow

100. Columbine Falls and Cave Canyon

Columbine Falls flows year-round, and is a wonderful place to visit as you near the end of your trip (Mile 274.4 L). Those who would like to attempt the difficult hike above the falls and into Cave Canyon will enjoy a 1/2 mile of flowing stream in a tight bouldery canyon.

To reach the falls is easy if the lake is full. The falls are tucked away in a small cove in the south corner of a bend of the river. This is the last bend in the Colorado before it crosses the massive down-drop of the Grand Wash Fault. When the lake is full, you can float over to the foot of the falls. If the lake is not within ten feet or so of full-pool, you will have to tie up at the upstream corner of the small cove. From here it may be possible to hike less than 1/4 mile to the falls right against the base of the cliff that defines the east side of this cove. It can be very brushy in here at times, or it can be impassable lake ooze.

To attempt the difficult hike up above the falls into Cave Canyon, you will need to climb up through a landslide on the west side of the drainage. You can do this from a couple of different spots.

If the lake is high enough to allow you to boat directly to the falls, you can start your hike from the base of this landslide. You will be able to climb up this steep slope, starting from a point only 100 yards or so north of the waterfall. Climb up to a bench above the cliffs that form the falls, and traverse along a thin path back into the drainage. Along the way you will cross a small seep spring, then reach an open bench of travertine amidst mature cat claw acacia. From this bench, continue around more cat claw, and then drop down the steep slope under a large overhanging section of travertine. This slope will lead right to the top of the falls. From here it's a wet 1/2 mile over pourover boulders and through some enchanting narrows to the Cave Canyon Spring.

If the lake is low, you'd do best to start your hike at the mouth of a small wash at about 274.5 L. You are right in the middle of a 3-mile section of Grand Canyon National Park on this side of the river, and are no longer on Hualapai Nation land when you hike away from shore. Climb up in elevation about 100 feet, and traverse east and then south the 1/4 mile back into Cave Canyon. You will traverse through the landslide just before you reach the top of the falls. There is a great view to the northwest of the very last section of Grand Canyon before the Canyon makes an abrupt transition into rolling basin-and-range country. Enjoy.

small high
water camp

Columbine Falls Camp
(low water)

Way Out

274

ELEVATION 1157

Columbine
Falls

Weeping

Cliffs

Spring

**Columbine Falls
And
Cave Canyon
Mile 274.25 L**

N

1/2 Mile

853

STAY INVOLVED!

River runners today, more then ever, need to stay informed about all wilderness river issues, from river health to river access. River Runners for Wilderness advocates for wilderness river protection and equitable access to those rivers for all river runners and those who care about wild lands. Your access to wilderness on the Colorado River in Grand Canyon is particularly threatened by those who would attempt to commercialize and motorize the majority of river access to the river. Your voice counts and you can be a part of protecting the river. See *www.RRFW.org* for more details on how you can get involved in protecting this great park and all wilderness rivers.